The Acquisition of a Second Writing System

ROSEMARY SASSOON

intellect™

Bristol, UK

First published in the UK in 1995 (reprinted in 2004) by
Intellect Books, PO Box 862, Bristol BS99 1DE, UK
First published in the USA in 1995 by
Intellect Books, ISBS, 920 NE 58th Ave. Suite 300, Portland, Oregon 97213-3786, USA

Consulting Editor:	Masoud Yazdani
Copy Editor:	Wendi Momen
Index:	Roy Davies
Book Design:	Pardoe Blacker Publishing (Lingfield, UK)

A catalogue record for this book is available from the British Library

ISBN 1-871516-43-9

Printed and bound in Great Britain by 4edge Ltd.

Contents

Acknowledgements

During the writing of this book I have been more grateful than I can adequately express for the advice and contributions from many of my friends. Some like Albertine Gaur, Chris Abbott, Fred Eade, Trilokesh Mukherjee and Fiona Ross have written sections specially for me. Others, who include Valerie Yule, Yoshiaki Nihei, Peter Lofting and Henry Kao have allowed me to reproduce from their theses, articles and papers. Illustrations have added immeasurably to my text, and I would like to express my thanks to the many individuals (and publishers who are individually acknowledged in each instance) who have allowed them to appear in this book. There is more to acknowledge - I cannot name all the many friends with whom I have discussed various issues - and who have generously given me their time and shared their expertise. At home, a great many of my husband John's ideas have found their way into this book, and my daughter Caroline has contributed considerably with key examples and sound advice. Finally, Michael Blacker has done far more than just design this book - I (and this volume) owe him a great deal in many ways.

Preface

The field of English as a second language is well researched and documented, but the equally important subject of how to acquire the Latin alphabet as a second writing system, or how to change from any particular writing system to another, has seldom been considered. An analytical approach to this subject is long overdue in our ever more mobile society, whether at the level of young immigrants, university students or business people.

In the English-speaking world, manuals and copybooks seem to assume that a suitable method to instruct a non-Latin writer, of any age, would be the same as that used to teach any English-speaking infant just entering school. In some cases this might be appropriate, but this way of thinking ignores both the special skills that experienced writers of some nationalities may have, as well as the special problems that might arise in other cases. It also ignores the retraining of the hand and sometimes the whole body that is needed where a new direction of writing is involved.

There are many factors involved, such as the age or stage of the learner. Adult attitudes to learning may differ from children's. When adults come to education they often have a purpose in mind. Therefore the adult tendency to select comes into play, and unless the teaching is in harmony with what they have selected, the teaching will be in vain. For children, particularly when they have just arrived in a new environment, a different approach might be needed. Some pupils might be reluctant learners, some traumatized, while at the other extreme, some may be especially diligent and ambitious.

The learner's level of skill in the first writing system, or the expectations from the second system would need to be taken into consideration, similarly whether two writing systems are being assimilated simultaneously. The more obvious question of whether the student is learning a more complex system or a simpler one than his or her first may also affect the situation. The problems facing those who need to learn a new language or writing system today are not confined to the new rules, characters or physical actions that they involve. Their difficulties may be exacerbated by the tension of upheaval, and more deeply in the case of those who are refugees from their native land. The situation can also be complicated by the pressures of anything from a new educational system, to a harassing business post.

Countries have different attitudes to writing and to education at large. There are those in some parts of the world who might consider the written aspect of a second language unimportant, even undesirable in the early stages, and an informal oral introduction to be vital. In other countries the motivation to acquire knowledge, allied to the discipline instilled by more structured educational systems, allows rapid progress, even at an early age. This is where written exercises can combine the alphabetic skills with consolidating certain aspects of language. Writing systems have created "civilizations" at the expense of memory. Those who come from less literate societies have a far greater capacity for memory than those who consider their education systems to be more advanced. This is something else to respect and build upon.

Any subject can be studied to show how we learn – and writing better than most, as it leaves a permanent trace. We need to search for what it is that triggers learning and what setting enables a child or older student to learn most easily. In a changing cultural pattern teachers need to be aware that some students may have been accustomed to acquiring information in different ways. If they come from an authoritarian culture, this might be the best way for them for a while at least, i.e. information conveyed and repeated in a formal setting. Conversely if they come from a freer educational environment, then enlightened discussion and experimentation are what they are used to, and may react best to initially. Not too much freedom should be allowed, however, as acquiring a second language and another writing system requires discipline.

We must extend what we know of the written trace to computer generated letters. Modern communication systems mean that internationally we are interacting at many levels, and this understanding of all our approaches to the written, printed and computer-generated word is becoming more and more important. I hope that this book will provoke discussion and lead to a better understanding of the many cross–cultural implications of written communication.

CHAPTER I

An Introduction to Writing Systems

The first part of this book tackles the subject of acquiring a second writing system – but this is not all. Handwriting, calligraphy, graphic communication or however you care to describe the recording of thoughts on paper is not just a matter of making black marks on a white sheet, not just a matter of learning a new code instead of the old one. To write we use our whole selves, our minds and our bodies. Our mark is a personal one, indicative of our character, our training and our culture. That is where the interesting part of changing writing systems begins to surface. In acquiring a second writing system you may be acquiring another cultural philosophy; you certainly are acquiring another set of physical movements and maybe with it a different way of thinking altogether.

From the other angle, the teachers', obviously they will need to be able to teach their own writing system, but they should also know a certain amount about some of the world's other writing systems. It helps to know something of the history and development of the cultures and their writing, although one cannot know about them all, nor need one necessarily know the languages in which they are all written. Something quite different is needed; a respect for other cultures, a sensitivity towards the needs of individual pupils, and a realization that above all this is a subject that cannot be taught in the same way to all second language students.

In too many English-speaking countries, Arabic pupils, along with Greek, Japanese, Israeli, Tamil, perhaps Spanish and several other nationalities might be found sharing the same classroom, as second language learners, at any age from five years old to fifty. However, they might all have different writing skills and what can best be described as different pluses and minuses when it comes to learning the Latin alphabet. Some will come from a much more complex writing system requiring more intense hand/eye

This was written for me by an elderly calligrapher in Hong Kong. He told me that it says 'Calligraphy (or handwriting) is the mirror of the mind. This reflects the whole content of this book, just as it did of *The Art and Science of Handwriting* where it was first reproduced. Here, however, this quotation, applied to a study of many writing systems, can be interpreted more widely to suggest that the influence of a culture and first writing system can pervade any subsequent ones, but that individuality will still show through, whatever the script.

coordination but very different rules, while others may have less dramatic but just as difficult changes to make. A similar way of thinking would profit those who only write the Latin alphabet and may be struggling to learn another writing system (in which case there are usually more minuses than pluses), or between any two other writing systems as well.

Analyzing writing systems

The formula that is suggested in this book is remarkably simple. It consists of analyzing the rules of the relevant writing systems and comparing them. These rules consist of matters concerning the characters or letters as well as the physical postures imposed on different systems by the writing implement (or tradition). At one time materials would also have had to be considered but this is unnecessary today when paper is universal. This idea is extended to include different levels of complexity of perception or production required by different systems, different concepts of beauty or perfection, and different attitudes to education in general. The intention is to make everyone concerned aware, in handwriting terms, where a writer has come from and where he or she is going.

When all the separate points have been teased out and are ready for comparison, you will have an idea of which aspects any particular country's pupils are likely to find most difficult – although there will be many individual differences within the general pattern. You will have a framework within which to plan your exercises which will enable you to contrast and compare those aspects that are likely to be either unfamiliar or confusing. It is a journey of discovery for both sides and a bridge between cultures and between teacher and pupil, with no limitations and no guarantees.

What is handwriting?

Handwriting is one of the subjects that we tend to take for granted. It is something that most people do so automatically that they seldom question what it is and how their own writing system works, much less anyone else's. Writing was the means by which the human race gradually developed a way of recording its languages. Long before abstract thoughts were recorded the need for factual records are believed to have been the motivation for the act of writing. Graphic signs on pottery or on cave walls were symbolic but not yet tied to language. The line between graphic communication, as perhaps represented by such symbols, and what we understand to be the earliest writing systems, such as cuneiform, depends on the point at which the symbol becomes standardized and fixed in relation to a specific word or phrase. There were various systems that were able to record bits and pieces of a language without being able to record all of it.

Classifying writing systems

Generally, writing systems can be classified according to what it is that they actually record. If it is ideas, then the words in which the ideas are expressed are less important, but there will need to be a large number of signs. If it is sounds, then these may be related to the language to be recorded in the form of syllables. Another way of recording sounds is to relate them not to words or whole syllables but to the separate sounds which make up the syllables. This is the system used by the alphabet, the simplest and probably the most flexible of the writing systems.

For convenience, writing systems can be roughly divided into ideographic, syllabic and alphabetic, recognizing that each system (and here punctuation and numerals are included) will have some elements of the others. Hieroglyphs and Chinese characters are examples of ideographic systems, although both have phonetic elements. They have characters that were first pictographic, expressing an object, which then came to represent an idea associated with that object. Eventually these came to represent a whole class of associated objects and ideas. Where different ideas are represented by the same sound a sign can be used as a determinant to indicate the category in which the it should be interpreted. (e.g. son/sun).

Butterworth and Yin (1991) include valuable insights into the organization of characters and their usage. They explain: 'Because Chinese is non-alphabetic, it is widely assumed that characters contain no sublexical information as to their pronunciation. This is not the case. Most characters, including the vast majority of common characters, contain a "phonetic radical" which can indicate how the character is to be pronounced.... Phonetic

Dipthongs
as in mediæval or
œsophagus

æ

œ

A thorn from an
handwriting scheme for
Icelandic schools by G
SE Briem

radicals are used in the creation of new characters, for loan words and can be used to construct pronounceable pseudo-words.'

Such subtleties enabled the Chinese writing system to expand indefinitely and survive successfully to the present day. Ideographic scripts are not language specific. This has enabled them to transcend language barriers, allowing civilizations to communicate long after they have separated or to unify national groups who retain their original languages.

Syllabic writing can be represented, historically, by cuneiform. One sign, in stages of decreasing reality as the system developed, represented one syllable. The signs soon ceased to have any relationship with the picture that they originally represented. Those sign values in cuneiform had to be memorized systematically, their rules were not very accurate and, as a result, such a system was cumbersome to write. Today, Japan uses two syllabaries: Katakana and Hiragana. Most of the symbols represent a single consonant followed by a single vowel sound.

Alphabetic systems use letters to represent sounds and pairs or groups of letters to represent more complex sounds. Different sound values can be given to the same letters. Alterations in sound values are even more evident within different languages. The Latin alphabet has expanded from the original set that served the Latin language well to include several letters to enable it to be used conveniently to represent different sounds in other tongues. The letters J, U and W were added during the Middle Ages. At the other extreme, some characters once used in written English have disappeared, such as the thorn, a Norse relic still used in Icelandic. More recently the dipthong has virtually been discontinued as a symbol. A variety of accents are used in order to obtain specific sounds in other Latin languages such as French or Spanish and still others, for example, for Germanic, Scandinavian and other tongues.

This is a fairly simplistic explanation of a complex subject. For instance Chinese ideograms and Egyptian hieroglyphs include phonetic elements. Those wanting a more detailed explanation of the complexities of ideographic, syllabic and alphabetic systems would do well to read *The Origins of Writing* (Harris 1986). He divided writing systems into five categories:

1 Alphabetic

2 Syllabic
3 Logographic
4 Pictographic
5 Ideographic

Diringer (1962) classified scripts in even more detail, explaining why he considered that some scripts designated as logographic should be considered analytic transitional scripts. He looked at writing systems from many different angles saying, for example: 'The struggle for survival is the principle condition for the existence of a script, as for many other things; and *on the whole,* barring severe interference of any kind, a script will evolve in the direction of simplicity and utility . . . and the fittest scripts will survive.' Diringer acknowledged that: 'There have been cases in which, without any external interference being visible, a script did not move towards greater utility and simplicity but developed in a quite contrary direction.' He cites Chinese as the obvious example, with its multiplicity of symbols of which, as he says, '3000–5000 are actually employed by Chinese scholars'.

Advantages and disadvantages
The simplicity of an alphabet is dependent on the fact that the number of of phonemes in most languages, according to Yule (1991), is limited to around 40, with a range of 12 to 60. This allows an alphabetic system to work with only a fraction of the characters that an ideographic or syllabic system employs. Yule sees other advantages: 'A new language or a previously unwritten one can be given a written form with relative ease, whereas creating a new symbol system is a major task. Since the letters are few they can be simple and distinctive, and easy to write and to copy. Input, output and storage in modern communications technologies present no problems for keyboards, printing and binary translation. Even though breakthroughs at first thought impossible have been made, keyboards and electronic technology for logographs remain more complex. Each word does not have to be learned separately, so the average person can reach a higher level of literacy with less effort than a learner of a logographic writing system. A writer can invent or misspell, and still communicate, whereas logographs are not so flexible.'

However, we cannot expect any meaningful relationship

between the sounds that the letters represent and the meaning of the word, such as you find with ideographs and sometimes in syllabaries. Moreover, unlike ideographs which can be understood independently from any specific language, the alphabet is not able to cross language barriers.

Languages and writing systems

It is impossible to separate entirely language from writing systems. Some languages are poorly served by writing systems which they have adopted (or had thrust upon them). Take, for example, the Latin alphabet which is used for so many diverse languages around the world. Obviously such problems are not confined to one set of languages, linked to any one alphabet. To go further, it could be asked whether any language can be fully represented by any alphabet, particularly as languages alter and expand much more flexibly and faster than writing systems. In some cultures the written form no longer reflects the spoken. As Gyoti Tamuli said of his native Assamese; 'Oral contact with Nagas and other different ethnic groups meant that the spoken form underwent changes: speech changed, but the writing system was left behind. There are as a consequence fewer consonantal sounds in the language today and more vowels. Changes are still going on and extra vowels are needed. The resulting difficulties are considerable.'

Terminology

Even when dealing with the Latin alphabet there are many terms which need defining. Some of them cause confusion because even those who teach their own writing systems do not fully understand them. There need to be terms to describe the different levels of writing: joined or separate, cursive or semi-cursive. These terms are relevant to many writing systems although they are sometimes used in slightly different ways. Then there are the complexities of the different models in use and the descriptions of the details of such letters. To someone learning an alphabet this matter of a model can be a major hurdle, somewhat similar to a local dialect in speech. The model that is picked up may depend on the national policy or simply the personal preference of the teacher, but it may have far-reaching consequences for the learner. The difference between national models and cultural concepts of letterforms is considerable, even within Europe for example. Someone having learned to write in one country who then moved to a school in another might have almost as much difficulty changing to a new national, district or even individual school model as someone learning a new writing system. The same situation no doubt exists within other writing systems. Handwriting is such an emotive subject, there is seldom agreement on stylistic matters.

How this book can help

This book commences by describing the rules and writing strategies of the Latin alphabet. This is to lay a foundation for understanding the factors that must be considered in any other writing system. Then the formula for comparing systems will be explained.

The techniques of each writing system need as much consideration as the characters themselves. The written trace is the product of our hands, so the different writing postures, which include paper position, penhold, etc. all need understanding. These factors may have to alter as another system is learned. All this will need explaining. While the techniques of many Eastern writing systems, including Arabic, have traditionally been strictly taught, these are beginning to be relaxed, producing problems that previously had not been present. The different writing tools and traditional writing materials have influenced the development of written characters. Some of these developments will be described, not only for general interest, but as a way of bridging the cultures and maybe providing imaginative ways out of the problems that may confront teachers of reluctant writers.

Attitudes all over the world are changing, however, and traditional tools are being discarded in favour of modern pens. They are used because of their availability and convenience, and sometimes as a symbol of rebellion against older cultural restrictions, but few people have considered the effects that they might have on writers' hands unless we develop more appropriate penholds for them.

Students may not need to write as quickly or, in many cases, be able to reach the speed that they can produce in their first language, yet speed and comfort must be high on the list of priorities. How this is achieved is dependent on the expertise of the teachers in their own system (the pupils' second) as well as their understanding of their pupils' writing posture in their first writing system. All this needs careful explanation and introduces factors that many people will not have considered at all in their past, either as writers themselves or as being part of their responsibility as a teacher.

The problems that afflict a percentage of all writers will begin to be revealed as soon as second language pupils begin to write. Some are the type of difficulties that would be evident in the writers' first writing system. These problems should be able to be recognized by experienced teachers whether or not they can comprehend the words written in the letters or characters involved. But everyone should be careful about using the usual criteria. The uncertainties of a new culture may be unexpectedly inhibiting and disturb any writer's trace. We need a whole new attitude to testing.

Although the main concern here is with the acquisition of a second writing system, this cannot be totally isolated from the creative tasks and other aspects of written language. It is a daunting and massive subject. I cannot begin to give all the answers, or even to deal with all the writing systems in use today, but I want to raise some of the vital issues that desperately need addressing.

INCORRECT MOVEMENT OF LETTERS

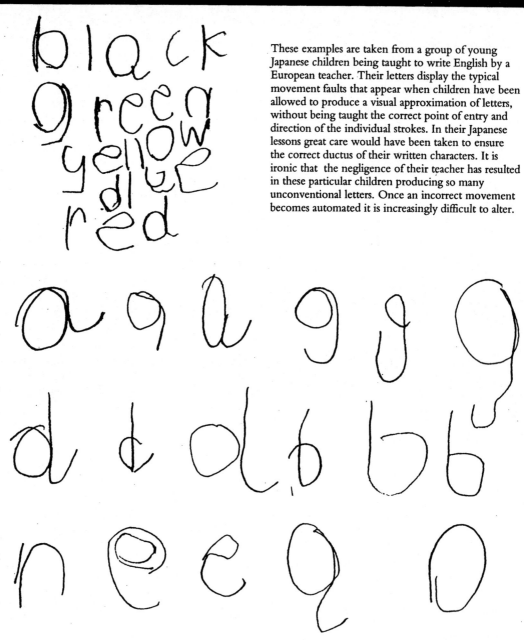

These examples are taken from a group of young Japanese children being taught to write English by a European teacher. Their letters display the typical movement faults that appear when children have been allowed to produce a visual approximation of letters, without being taught the correct point of entry and direction of the individual strokes. In their Japanese lessons great care would have been taken to ensure the correct ductus of their written characters. It is ironic that the negligence of their teacher has resulted in these particular children producing so many unconventional letters. Once an incorrect movement becomes automated it is increasingly difficult to alter.

CHAPTER 2

Comparing the Rules of Writing Systems

Writing is a taught skill with different rules within different cultures. Some rules seem to be purely arbitrary, some came about because of the tools and materials that were available at the time that they were developing, and some rules became necessary as the systems, languages or even writing styles themselves developed.

First teachers – or students – must be clear about the rules that govern their own writing system, before they can begin to compare them with those of another. These rules concern such matters as direction, movement, height differentials and spacing.

The rules that govern the Latin alphabet are:
· The direction of writing is from left to right.
· There are conventional points of entry and direction of the strokes that make up the letters. This determines the movement or ductus of the letters.
· Letters are of different heights and these heights are constant in their relation to each other.
· There are two sets of letters: capital letters and small letters.
· Letters and words are spaced adequately.

People who only know their own writing system might assume that there is a right way and a wrong way to write, or even one way that works best for the human body. But this is patently not so. Take any one of these rules in turn and compare it within different writing systems, and the variations become obvious. Handwriting does not work properly for the writer until it has been automated and it is difficult to be analytical about an automatic action. This method of analysing the different rules of a writing system will help you to understand your own way of writing as well as pointing the way to understanding other systems.

DIRECTION OF WRITING

Above: **Confused directionality – an example of Boustrophedon.**
This Japanese child, (from the same set used to demonstrate movement problems on
p 16) was asked to copy the names of colours off the board. He first proceeded from
left to right along the line and then started back from right to left. Notice how
many of the letters are reversed when starting from the end of the line backwards.
This way of writing is called Boustrophedon (the way the ox ploughs) and was used
in several writing systems early in their development.

Directionality

The other two examples appeared in an exercise book from Hong Kong. The
numerals are aligned from right to left and top to bottom in two lines.
Measurements in English are printed sideways proceeding downwards.

19	17	15	13	11	9	7	5	3	1
雨	狗	海	狀	布	果	草	汗	耳	牙

20	18	16	14	12	10	8	6	4	2
溫習	風	車	魚	門	溫習	豆	花	足	舌

作爲學校的用書，本書使我們引以爲傲的，是它在兒
童敎育專家設計下，擁有比同類書更多的優點：豐富的內
容，循序漸進的編排、富吸引力的圖畫以及更適合兒童的
開本（15.5cm×13cm）。

Direction

It is thought that originally most of the world's writing systems were written from right to left or in vertical columns starting from the right. Some subsequently altered, possibly influenced by their writing materials. Even though the situation is gradually changing, as it is in Japan, for instance, right-to-left is still the direction for major systems such as Arabic and Hebrew. In some scripts directional ambiguity is still found. Eade (1992) provides an example of Tifinagh, which literally means 'the letters of the the Tuareg alphabet'. The script can be written vertically from bottom to top, horizontally from left to right or boustrophedon (in both directions on alternate lines). This script is used with the Tamasahek language in western Niger, northern Burkina Faso, eastern Mali, southern Algeria and south west Libya.

}⊙꞊· ⊙ꞁⵍ+
Ⅱ#ⵎ꞊+ +ꞁ
ꞁⵔ꞊ ꞊·+⊙꞊
⌐ⵔ ⵎꞌⵔꞌⵐꞌ ꞊·E
ꞁE+⊙Ⅱ\꞊

Some letters of the the Tuareg alphabet. From Eade (1992).

Direction of writing in Tifinagh can be vertical, horizontal, or in two dimensions.

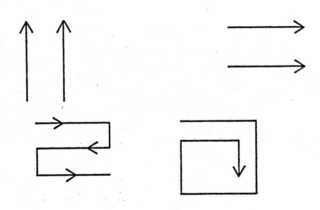

The kind of directional confusion illustrated by the child on the opposite page gives us an idea of the difficulty that might face writers when having to alter the direction of their writing. Most writers adapt fairly easily but at what cost to the fluency and speed of their early writing we can only guess. A simple way of assisting writers in such a situation would be to give them a strip of coloured paper placed at the point where the line of writing should start. Arrows indicating direction might also help in the first instance.

SEQUENCE AND DIRECTION OF STROKES

			From *Learn Hindi in 30 Days*, Srinivasachari (1979)
			From *The Hebrew Letter*, David (1990) reprinted by permission of the publisher, Jason Aronson Inc., Northvale, NJ.
			From an Arabic copybook
			From two different unnamed Chinese copy sheets.

Ductus: The way in which a script is written, its speed and care of execution and form of letters.

Brown 1990

Ductus or movement

Most writing systems have strict rules about the order and direction in which the strokes that make up their characters should be written. These rules are important because they ensure that however fast the characters are written and, to a certain extent, however many personal deviations of form occur, the writing remains legible. The prescriptions for the point of entry and direction of strokes of similar shapes of characters may differ among writing systems. As the illustrations opposite show, there are many different strategies for indicating the point of entry and direction and sequence of the strokes, which together govern the movement of letters or characters.

Another way of indicating point of entry and direction of stroke iillustrated in tracing and tracking exercises from Sassoon (1990).

Those teaching children (or adults, for that matter) to write in any language or writing system may be tempted to allow them to reproduce a visual approximation of a letter or character rather than the strict order and movement of the individual strokes. An example of such teaching is illustrated by the writing of young Japanese children on p. 16.

This method of teaching may allow pupils to express themselves more quickly in writing, but may also have a disastrous effect later on. As writing is a physical act, any aspect of it quickly becomes automated, and when practised, becomes increasingly difficult to alter. Once a letter or character is incorrectly automated it means that the writer must bring the act of writing back into conscious thinking to correct it. It is always worth spending the time to teach students the correct movements that apply to whatever writing system is being taught. Exercises can be devised to show the movement (visual exercises), to allow the pupil to feel the movement (kinaesthetic exercises) as well as orally describing the direction and sequence of strokes. In this way the teacher is reinforcing this vital instruction in three modes. This is a good idea because some people learn best through one method and some another.

HEIGHT DIFFERENTIALS AND PROPORTIONS

From a Chinese copy sheet illustrating position and proportion within a square.

Tamil and Thai illustrated by students.

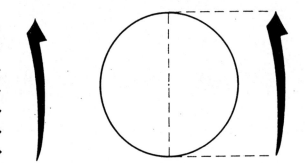

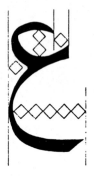

Selected letters illustrating the method of Ibn Muqlah (d 940). From Safadi (1978), *Islamic Calligraphy*.

Below: Proportions and alignment of Arabic from a writing book for children.

Height differentials and proportions

Some writing systems have their heights clearly defined between four lines, some between two and others have no height differentials in the sense that the Latin alphabet has, for example those whose characters are contained within a square. Within those squares, however, other rules of height and proportion must be rigorously adhered to. Fok and Bellugi (1986) explain the spacial architecture of characters this way: 'The grapheme components of the Chinese character are arranged within a square frame. In most characters this frame is partitioned in a number of different ways, with components occurring side by side, in horizontal layers, in quadrants etc. The components are themselves made up of a variety of strokes which derive from a limited set of possibilities, applied in a relatively fixed order' In other writing systems, Arabic calligraphy for example, the heights of letters vary according to their position in the word, and while many alphabets are aligned to a baseline, some Indian scripts hang from a top line.

> The legibility of writing depends on correct height differentials. This is because fluent readers usually scan the shape of words to extract their meaning. When teaching any writing system the heights and proportions of letters or characters will need to be explained carefully. In the Latin alphabet this could be achieved in a variety of ways. A teacher could start by listing together letters of the same height then devise suitable exercises, e.g. bdfhkl (ascending strokes), fgjpqy (descending strokes), tf (exceptions to the rule). Guidelines may be needed. Use a baseline at least. In some cases all four heights may need to be indicated. Guidelines should be appropriate to the size of the writing of any particular student.

lili lplli lijil iltjtli

bag fit top fly

Exercises can be devised to progress from pattern to letter pattern to increasingly complex words.

Quattrolinear script: A script which by the incorporation of ascenders and descenders occupies four lines.

Bilinear script: A script whose letters are confined between two lines – the head and base lines.

Brown 1990

CAPITAL LETTERS

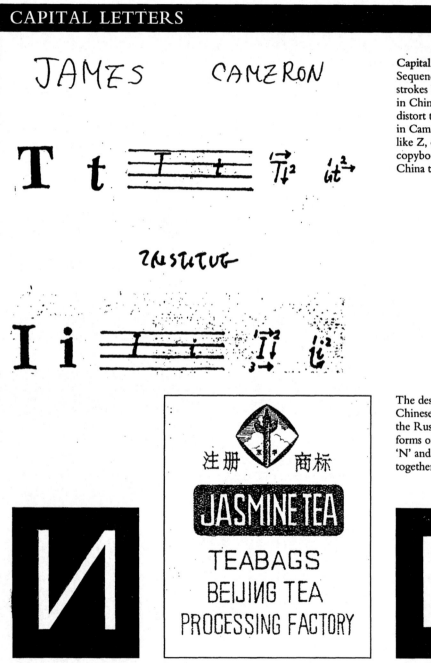

Capital letters
Sequencing horizontal strokes before vertical, as in Chinese characters may distort the letter. See the E in Cameron which looks like Z, or I in Institute. A copybook used in south China teaches this way.

The designer of this Chinese tea bag confused the Russian and Latin forms of the capital letter 'N' and used them both together.

The letter 'E' suffers considerable indignities particularly when Chinese children write the horizontal strokes before the vertical ones.

Sets of letters

The concept of two sets of letters, capitals and small letters, is by no means universal. Some alphabets, such Cyrillic, use mainly capital letters in print, but both for handwriting. Other scripts such as Arabic and Hebrew traditionally did not have capital letters at all. Some writing systems get over the problem, at least in type, in a different way. Bolder weights of letters, or characters in the case of Chinese or Japanese, are used for headings and in other situations where capitals might otherwise occur.

The capital letters in the Latin alphabet are not usually expected today to join either to a following capital letter or to a small one. Therefore their ductus is less important, unless it so disrupts the form of the letters that they become difficult to recognize. Sequencing horizontal strokes before vertical, as in Chinese characters, may distort the letters enough to do this. See the E in Cameron which looks like Z, or I in Institute. Close inspection of a copybook used in south China demonstrates this stroke sequence, so it is not surprising that the students adopt it.

Dd Ee Ff Mm Nn

Students learning the Latin alphabet need exercises that not only help them to recognize the two different forms of capital and small letters, but also the different movements involved. Most capital letters are fairly obvious if the writer follows the usual rule of starting vertical strokes at the top; however others are neither logical nor necessarily standard in their movements. The letter M, for instance, is sequenced three ways in as many English copybooks, yet none of them affect the legibility adversely. The pairs of letters which seem to cause most trouble are Dd, Ee, Ff, Mm and Nn. It is not difficult to devise ways of letting students compare and contrast these letters in such a way that they soon become familiar.

For students, those from China for instance, who might be needing to use the Latin and Cyrillic alphabets at the same time, the capital letter N presents an additional point of confusion. The diagonal strokes are written in opposite directions.

MIRROR IMAGE

Mirror image is a particular problem of the Latin alphabet which was designed (or has developed) using a limited range of strokes. As a result several pairs of letters are mirror images of each other. They can cause problems for those whose first alphabet it is, as well as for those learning English as a second language and writing system. Mirror image discrimination is particularly difficult for children, as it is not required in other aspects of learning.

These pattern and letters come from Sassoon (1991) *Handwriting Book*, Children's English, Linguaphone. They illustrate the two series of letters that cause most problems because they are mirror images of each other. Tactile as well as visual exercises may be used to help pupils, in addition to oral descriptions of the differences.

Spacing

Most writing systems have a means of separating words or characters, but the rules are by no means the same. Traditionally, languages with definite prefixes or suffixes did not require spaces between words in order to be deciphered. The Latin alphabet only relatively recently developed word spacing partly as a consequence of its use in writing languages where the structure does not denote clearly the beginnings and endings of words. The letters of the Trajan Column, for example, which are still considered as perhaps the finest examples of such Roman capitals, are inscribed with no word spaces. Those whose own system works on a different principle, such as Chinese, may have initial difficulty with completely different systems of word spacing.

The phrases IHAVE and 'THEGREATWALL' appear without word spaces. This illustrates the problem that word spacing might pose to Chinese writers whose own system involves a different concept – or, as in this case, for printers – who might not even understand the language that they are setting.

There is a simple rule for those who need help with word spacing. It is that the usual space should be that of a letter of the size that is being written. This follows the rule of the keyboard with which most people are familiar. The tradition in teaching had been to tell children to use a thumb or finger to measure the space between words, but this can lead to over-wide gaps between words as fingers and thumbs grow while writing tends to decrease in size with age.

JOINING LETTERS

Correct Writing and Joining of Letters

1. In joining letters be sure to set *л*, *М*, and *я* off from preceding letters. For example:

хотя must not be written *хотя*

или must not be written *или*

Note that *хотя* could be mistaken for хопя and *или* for иги. This confusion can be avoided by beginning the letters *я* and *л* with the short hook

2. Letters can be written continuously without a break, except when *л*, *М*, or *я* follow *о* . For example:

моя, полка, потом

3. Note the differences between *г* and *л*. Always make the *ш* with three loops; do not make it like the English *w*. The tails in *ц* and *щ* must be considerably shorter than that of *у*.

4. In order to avoid confusion between *т* and *ш*, they are frequently written thus:

т̅ (т), *ш̲* (ш).

Some details of joins in the Cyrillic script. From *Simplified Russian Grammar*, Fayer (1987).

Cursive: A rapid ductus, with fewer penlifts and with devices to increase speed, such as the linking of letters and perhaps loops.

Brown 1990

Separate letters or joined letters

Some writing systems, such as Latin and Cyrillic, have both separate letters and joined ones. Others such as Hebrew traditionally had separate letters, while Arabic is usually considered a joined hand. These differences cannot be explained precisely because so many rules are being broken worldwide. Moreover the term 'cursive' itself seems inadequate to describe forms within a writing system, much less between them. Scripts which are eventually expected to join are usually taught in the separate forms first and then learners are shown how to join the letters. Sometimes the letters remain the same, but some may need to alter in order to join satisfactorily. This has occurred several times throughout the centuries in the Latin alphabet. Most writers take penlifts during long words (whether consciously or unconsciously) and this results in what might be better called a semi-joined hand. This has partly been a consequence of the dramatic alterations in writing implements over recent years. Modern pens require different penholds and need the hand to be supported on the table, so alphabets that have been considered cursive, if examined, might reveal penlifts mid-word. Penlifts allow the hand to have a necessary rest after the completion of a complex series of movements. Speed is now a priority, and the traditional training of many centuries is being relaxed and finally ignored

To alter a script from separate letters or characters to joined ones usually means only that the writer keep the writing implement on the paper between letters or between elements of characters in a prescribed way. However, as separate letters become part of a flowing sequence, personal variations and shortcuts occur spontaneously and some of the forms inevitably alter in subtle ways. In Arabic, some letters are not intended to be joined while others alter their appearance when they are joined. Others have different forms in the initial, medial and final positions. How, therefore, should one define cursive other than from its Latin root meaning 'running' – and why is it used to describe continuously joined writing anyhow when Roman cursives themselves did not join much? Is it then a principle of various writing systems, a habit which can vary from writer to writer, depending on the writing implement or the length of words within the language employed, or is it a particular style or, above all, a desire to increase speed?

Other matters to consider

Greek writers learning the Latin alphabet have a somewhat
different problem. They have to contend with the fact that some
of their capital letters represent a different sound in languages
which use the Latin alphabet. The use of accents or diacritics may
cause initial difficulty for those who are not used to them in their
own language or writing system. Both these points come into
slightly different categories but cannot be ignored and remind us
that the act of writing itself cannot be divorced from other aspects
of written language.

A label from a water
bottle in both Greek
and English – so similar
yet strangely puzzling to
the reader.

Similarities and dissimilarities

From these simple statements a pattern is beginning to be built up.
Where a rule is absent or different in the second writing system
then a particularly clear explanation will be needed. Quite likely
specific exercises will be needed to make the assimilation easier. A
rule that has only a slight difference may appear to be a simple
alteration, but may present more difficulty for far longer. For
example, if a character in one system appears similar to one in
another but has a different point of entry and direction of stroke, it
can be very confusing and continue to plague the writer even after
suitably designed exercises to compare and contrast the two
characters.

The company logo
illustrates the linguistic
differences even more
clearly.

   If writers have no experience of any particular aspect of writing
then they cannot be expected to pick it up without a clear
explanation. This analytical way of looking at similarities and
dissimilarities between writing systems makes you think more
deeply about your own. This is important because unless the
teacher has a clear understanding, then this vital explanation will
not be forthcoming.

instances that illustrate how the rules that relate to specific writing systems differ. The next step would then be to devise suitable exercises. Some ideas are shown in this chapter and many more in the next one where students have worked with me. They have identified the specific problems that they faced when learning a second writing system.

This chapter is not meant to provide standard material for anyone to copy. This would be counter-productive as exercises must relate precisely to the two writing systems involved. The illustrations show how easy it is to devise simple exercises to explain and then deal with whatever problems arise. Ideally, a similar method should be used to teach from the beginning by comparing the rules of the two relevant systems and anticipating those features which are likely to be troublesome. After a very short time, such a method of teaching would become automatic.

More about teaching

Learning a second writing system may have some similarities with learning a first one, but it has also many differences. These should be recognized and built on in any teaching material. Both the age and the stage of the child will be likely to differ. This situation is not now one of young children struggling to make a pencil obey them. The students will be capable of producing an accurate written trace. Moreover hand-eye coordination is likely to be better developed in those with more complex writing systems than the Latin alphabet. In that case, any preliminary exercises should be specialized and sufficiently sophisticated for the pupil to take them seriously. There will be none of the problems of children not understanding the purpose of the task that confronts them. To the contrary, there will be considerable self-motivation to progress as fast as possible and to keep up with the pace of oral work. This is a good place to bring in another important point: although this aspect of handwriting has been ignored in Europe since the days of the great educationist Montessori, there is a certain amount of evidence to suggest that by forming the letters by hand you are internalizing the word as you write. Montessori showed that by teaching handwriting at an early age before teaching reading, the one skill led on to the other.

In second language acquisition the importance of reinforcing oral

In second language acquisition the importance of reinforcing oral
work by written work is usually stressed, but the exercises that are
presented are seldom worked out in a structured manner. Far too
often they consist of rhymes or sentences that do little to further an
intelligent student's knowledge of the language. It is time to focus
attention on a systematic method of teaching that will enable those
competent and motivated young pupils to acquire and automate
some of the aspects of the language at the same time as learning the
writing system. It has already been mentioned that when learning a
second language, even without a second writing system, there is a
need to automate new letter combinations. The exercises that are
illustrated here come from a set of books designed for Chinese
children learning English. Common letter combinations are set
into words of varying complexity. Comparatives and superlatives
combine essential elements of language with the repetition of letter
strings that benefit the motor aspects of learning the alphabet.

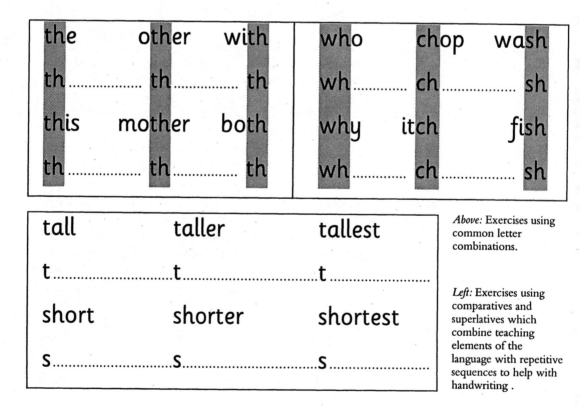

Above: Exercises using common letter combinations.

Left: Exercises using comparatives and superlatives which combine teaching elements of the language with repetitive sequences to help with handwriting .

Languages and writing systems

Before we leave the general area of exercises, there is something to say about the relationship between languages and the characters that represent them — something that can create even more barriers if it is not explained. Some alphabets, such as Latin, are easy to read but difficult to pronounce once they are used other than for their original language. Other scripts are difficult to learn because of the complexities of the languages that they were designed to represent; however, once learned they are easy to pronounce.

Let me give you an example of how confusing English spelling or pronunciation can be to someone learning the language unless the reasons are explained. A mature post-graduate student stopped to talk to me one day at a certain university renowned for its Institute of Education. An Arabic writer, he told me that he had had little difficulty with the writing system but found the rationale behind the spelling and pronunciation of English quite incomprehensible. This is not my subject, but it was impossible to ignore his trouble. He was experiencing the problems caused by the use of an alphabet designed for the Latin language being used for another complex language which includes sounds, and therefore letter combinations, from Anglo-Saxon, Celtic, Norse and of course Latin and French and even Greek. His face lit up and out came the expected question: 'Why did not anyone explain it this way when I was learning English — where can I get a book on this subject?' I sent him off to the university library although the clearest illustration that I have found came from a modest book for children. In her preface Pollock (1978) says, 'This book is intended for teachers — in class, in remedial sessions and teaching English to foreigners — so that they may give their pupils the kind of insight into the English language that will help them to improve their spelling'. She illustrates her point with a wonderful page of war cries using appropriate letter combinations from the various invading hordes that occupied Britain and left their marks on the language. All the different sounds have to be represented somehow by the 26 letters of the alphabet.

FROM SEPARATE LETTERS TO JOINED LETTERS

Tinkerbell whose kennel caught fire.
suffered very serious injuries.

This competent 12-year-old boy from Malaysia had a neat print script, but was not joining his letters.

ililil ililil
ill ill ill
hill hill hill hill
mill mill mill mill muuu
minimuuu minimum a au ai an
diu din din kin kin eut eut
the the the iu iu n in ooou
oooo ooh ooh ooh uheu le
bore bore room room room la
cat ca cau cat cat cat.

Some simple exercises quickly showed him how to join up.

Tinkerbell whose kennel caught fire
suffered very serious injuries.

The difference in the maturity and efficiency of his writing is clear.

Teachers' note: The first exercise uses the simplest letters that join from the base. This gives the pupil confidence to tackle top joins and finally the reverse joins. Pupils should be told that they need not join every letter all the time, but that they may take penlifts in the middle of long words.

CHAPTER 3

Observations or Statistics: Which Help us Most?

This chapter is more concerned with how to identify specific problems and devise exercises to deal with them than to present data. However, it provides an opportunity to compare two ways of investigating the prevalence and types of errors that might occur when acquiring a second writing system.

In a formal research situation, it is possible to set a test text and scrutinize it for the incidence of any visible faults. These faults can then be tabulated and submitted to statistical analysis in the hope of reaching certain conclusions about the likely problems of any set of writers. This is a complex and time-consuming operation and would need a large sample in order to reach any useful conclusions. There is, however, a different way of going about such enquiries. This is by consulting pupils at certain stages when they are learning a new writing system and getting them to discuss their problems. A pattern of likely difficulties should soon emerge.

I have found the less scientific method of observation and questioning more useful than formal research in understanding the difficulties that face students embarking on a second writing system. This does not mean that I do not value cross-cultural research. To the contrary, far too little of it is undertaken and this issue is discussed at the end of the chapter.

Observation and questioning

Students who are fairly advanced in learning a second writing system are often in the best position to explain to us what their specific problems are or were – which letters they have found most difficult to learn and any other matters that might have arisen. From the examples shown here, any experienced teacher should be able to work out the exercises that would help another student in the same position. Such exercises would need to compare similarities and differences and allow sufficient repetition for the student to automate any awkward or misunderstood features.

A THAI TEENAGER AND HIS VARIATIONS

เรียนเกี่ยวกับภูมิประเทศของออสเตรเลียและ นิวซีแลนด์

The Thai alphabet written out by a student.

ก ข ค ฅ ง ฆ ฅ ช ซ ฌ ฎ ฏ ฐ ฒ.

Lettters that might cause problems because they resemble letters from the Latin alphabet but have different starting or finishing points.

The boy enlarged the three which had caused him most problems.

He will go my way

Two characters from the alphabet above.

Two adaptations which he used in English as the letter 'w', a traditional one and a teenage one.

Write a character analysis of Denis

She could not afford to send him

Thus Denis was sent to a. school

his mother though aware of this was

it. Dennis was not happy at

Several other of his letters were difficult to recognize, specially, 's' (see 'was' above).

From a Thai children's ABC teaching them to write the typographic form of letter 'a'. This may explain one of the problems of the boy shown opposite.

A Thai student explains letters that resemble each other

A young Thai student wrote out his alphabet for me. He had no difficulty in picking out the letters that look the same in the two alphabets, Thai and Latin, but whose strokes either start at a different point or are written in a different direction. His attitude was typical of those whose work appears in this chapter. I found that students coming from countries where handwriting is taken seriously, where they have been competently taught the structure and ductus of their own writing systems, seem to take an analytical approach to an alphabet that, sadly, English-speaking children no longer have.

This boy warmed to the subject of writing and began to explain certain teenage preferences for what he described as 'trendy' letterforms. He showed me the two forms of the letter which resembles 'w'. If the teenage form was used in English it could make a word difficult to decipher. Previously written examples from his English books showed up a few more problem letters, such as the 's'. Teachers need to be aware of the letters that might be a problem for Thai (and other) students. They can then devise exercises to compare and contrast those that resemble each other but whose strokes have a different point of entry or direction.

A teacher would need a fair knowledge of letterforms to be able to discuss the characteristics of letters, in the way that would be needed in this case (and many other similar ones) without being destructive. As described in chapter 5, it is quite usual, and not necessarily undesirable, for writers to retain a certain flavour of a first alphabet in their second. It is really a matter of how far the writer can go without losing the recognizability of the letter. In this case a teacher would not want to frighten the boy into using the complete basic form of 's', as taught to a five-year-old, but would need to show how its essential character requires a change in direction and a completion of the final stroke to make the letter easily recognizable. Then it would be possible to work together with different variations of this or any other letter which might need to be tackled, to find one to suit the writer – first in a separate form and then joined. It may help to do what has been done here – to enlarge the details of the relevant letters.

KOREAN HANGUL EXPLAINED IN STAGES

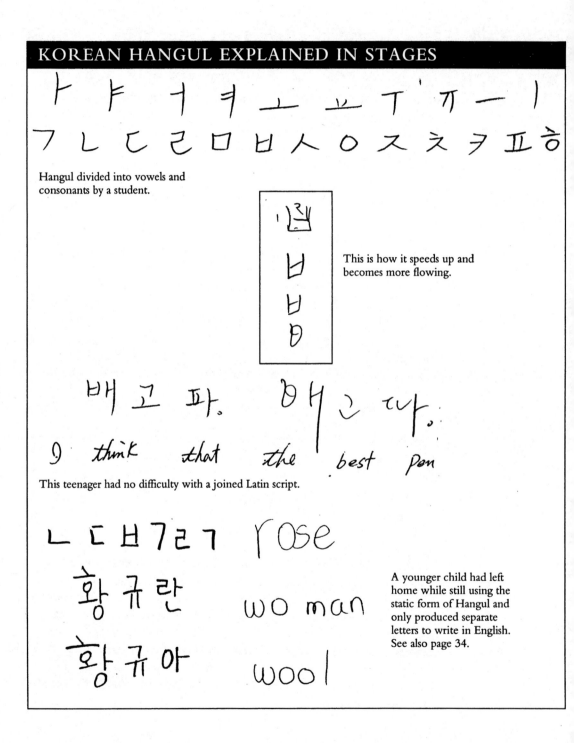

ㅏ ㅑ ㅓ ㅕ ㅋ ㅗ ㅛ ㅜ ㅠ ㅡ ㅣ

ㄱ ㄴ ㄷ ㄹ ㅁ ㅂ ㅅ ㅇ ㅈ ㅊ ㅋ ㅍ ㅎ

Hangul divided into vowels and consonants by a student.

This is how it speeds up and becomes more flowing.

배 고 파. 애ㄹ 따.

I think that the best pen

This teenager had no difficulty with a joined Latin script.

ㄴ ㄷ ㅂ ㄱ ㄹ ㄱ rose

황 규 란

wo man

황 규 아

wool

A younger child had left home while still using the static form of Hangul and only produced separate letters to write in English. See also page 34.

Korean pupils illustrate the issues involved in joining
A Korean teenager showed the forms of consonants and vowels and demonstrated how static forms became more flowing. She had a younger child under her care and explained how different it was for him to learn the rather formal cursive they were taught in their English lessons at the school in Hong Kong, as he had left Korea before reaching a relaxed, flowing stage of writing.

When pupils have not reached a mature stage in their first writing system there will be little understanding of the slight alterations in form that occur between separate letters and joined ones. Nor will the writer necessarily understand that in most cases it is a matter of having the confidence to keep the pen or pencil on the paper when proceeding within a character or from where one letter ends to where the next begins. The way that the small school that both these pupils attended used older pupils from the same country to help younger ones was sensitive and efficient. It helped both age groups – the older ones gained stature and became even more analytical about their own writing, and the young ones, who knew that their mentors had faced the same problems and solved them, reacted positively.

the hill
Letters with exit strokes

the hill
Letters without exit strokes

The younger pupil illustrates how the use of static print script letters acts against the best interests of those learning to write the Latin alphabet, whether as a first writing system or a second. These simplified letters may be helpful in the task of letter recognition which is part of learning to read, but not for handwriting which involves movement and requires that a physical movement is automated. The straight strokes of print script require the writer to alter pressure and direction before they can join. Letters with exit strokes make life easier for learners by building in the necessary space between letters, as well as promoting a relaxed and flowing action This young pupil would profit from similar exercises to those illustrated by the Malaysian student on page 34.

PUPILS FROM SRI LANKA AND STYLISTIC PROBLEMS

 බ අ ඨ

This student would be competent in any writing system.

2 3 2 3

අ බ ඩ ඏ ඝ ඨ ක න

2. The girl who sits next to
me in class . is my cousin.

2 The tape -recorder was made in Japan.
My uncle lent it to me.

A less mature student reflects the roundness of her first writing system in her separate letters. She had trouble with the narrowness of this cursive model.

nail-clippers Entry strokes troubled her.

Pupils from Sri Lanka illustrate problems with certain models
Sri Lankan children in several locations were unanimous in telling
me that their characters were the most difficult to write and that
everything about the Latin alphabet was easy in comparison – that
is one positive point of view anyhow. This might apply to separate
letters which, in most cases that I saw, were rounded and relaxed,
reflecting the rounded shapes of their own alphabet. However,
when it came to joins, those same children had difficulty in
conforming to the narrow format of the taught cursive. Two
pupils' work appears on the opposite page. The top one appears
competent and produced a well controlled trace in both the letters
and the numerals. It is the second child whose writing suggested
problems. Perhaps a few difficulties might be expected from the
over-large and not very well formed writing in her first alphabet.
As it happens she produced a clear, if rather immature print script,
The joined up example which appears below is deceptive. The
original is coated in ridges of correction fluid (which proves its
worth by disguising all these alterations when the example is
reproduced). The unfortunate pupil was being made to follow a
very condensed model and was having great difficulty in confining
the generous proportions of the letters which came naturally to
her. The pupil showed that the entry strokes were yet another
problem – a quite unnecessary one too.

*Teachers worldwide need to be aware of the problems that certain
models may cause for learners. While some students may be
competent enough to adapt to any proportion or detail of letters, others may
experience real difficulties and deserve that they should be given more
freedom. Some students have told me that aesthetically they prefer the
complexity of traditional continuous cursive – and they can manage it,
entry strokes and all, but the idea that efficient simplified letters are more
appropriate today is spreading. The pupil opposite would certainly have
profited from this attitude. We cannot expect all children to be equally
competent as writers, even in cultures where handwriting has a high profile.
Look out for those who indicate problems in their first writing system,
expect more trouble and take special care of them.*

A BURMESE WRITER DISPLAYS EARLY TENSIONS

ေအာင် မျိုး ေသာ ်ဦး : ြမင် ေသာ ်ေဒ ်ကို ြကည်

I live in happy valley yuk sau street

ြမ ်ဗ ်မ ်မ ်ှ ်ဗ ်ှ ်ေအာင် မျိုး : ေသာ .

I have been learning english for six years

This boy had no apparent problems with either separate or joined letters.

Touch Tasts Tongue

Maung

H.K Island

Some unusual capital letters.

H

Write the following into the shorter form.

There were signs of tension in his earlier exercise books. It has affected alignment.

A Burmese pupil's book revealed alignment troubles

The sample that this boy proudly wrote revealed very few problems. He had a pleasantly rounded writing which reflected the proportions of his Burmese letters. He had made the transition from separate letters to joined ones very skilfully. When asked if he had encountered any problems he proudly answered 'no'. There were a few minor 'differences' in his capital letters but these might be a result of the model that he had been taught. I had to go back to the beginning of one of his exercises to find any indications of how difficult he had found the new alphabet. It was the alignment of the letters and whole words that alerted me, as it would any observant teacher. Two possibilities arise from the unevenness of his work. One is that he had difficulty with the height differentials, in which case guidelines might have helped him. However the whole appearance of his work suggested something quite different. I think that the 'jumpiness' of his writing was likely to be the result of tension as he strove to conquer the new skills and achieve the high standard that he was setting himself.

As well as the obvious problems, teachers need to be sensitive to the tensions that are likely to be present in so many children who have been uprooted from their homes and are having to learn new skills in alien surroundings. Handwriting can be a valuable diagnostic aid and the pupils' growing confidence will be mirrored in their writing, as will their unhappiness or inadequacies. Tension of the body is transmitted via the hand to the written trace and makes itself evident in various ways such as unevenness of spacing, size and alignment, as well as unevenness of pressure. The tense jagged strokes that result from tense hands are easier to spot. Such matters should not necessarily be talked about, certainly not in such a way that might be construed as criticism and further sap a pupil's confidence. As in this case, they will, with luck, solve themselves.

GREEK WRITING; SIMILARITIES AND DIFFERENCES

Το Όνομα μου είναι Χριστιάννα.

My name is Kristianna

I get mixed up with the greek

and English e. Εε

A Greek girl explained her confusion over the letter 'e' which is not vital as both
forms are recognised and used in English.

α β γ δ ε 3 η θ ι κ λ μ ν ξ

ο π ρ σ τ υ φ χ ψ ω

Comparing the two alphabets.

p q r s t u v w x y z

Mount u u u Mount

Comparing and correcting the letter 'u'.

ρ ρ ρ ρ   ρ is easier

Comparing the movement of 'p' and the Greek 'r' (ρ).

A Greek girl compares two similar alphabets

This Greek girl in a London primary school was bi-lingual and write both alphabets equally well, so she was in a good position to tell me what her problems had been. Her first answer pinpointed confusion over the two forms of the letter 'E' or 'e'. As it happens this is not very important as far as legibility goes, because both forms are easily recognizable and freely used by English writers. When she wrote out both alphabets another, more important point of confusion became apparent. She was using the Greek form of the letter 'u' when writing in English. This lacks the final stroke required by the Latin letter so, although it would be recognisable in its separate form, it would be difficult for it to be joined in such a way as to be easily legible within a word. She quickly understood what was needed and rewrote the word 'mount', even saying that it worked better that way. I wondered if the resemblance of the Greek letter 'r' to the Latin 'p' worried her, or whether she got confused by the different point of entry or direction of stroke, but she told me that this presented no problem

Other problems that might face Greek pupils learning to write in English have been discussed elsewhere, but this example has several lessons for teachers. What one child may find difficult another may not. It is for the teacher to be on the lookout for possible points of confusion, and adults should not be worried about discussing such matters with any available pupil. It is the best (and in some cases the only) way to learn. Teachers cannot be expected to be conversant with details of all the writing systems that they may encounter in our truly multi-cultural schools. In this Greek girl's school 29 languages were spoken. I would like to suggest more ways in which a teacher might 'use' an intelligent child such as this one in the classroom. Surely it is valuable for the whole class to learn about other writing systems. Any demonstrations could be prefaced by the statement 'Are we not lucky to have someone clever enough to show us how to write in Chinese or Arabic', for instance. A whole class project on the subject of writing systems of the world would be valuable for everyone. It could also give confidence and status to those whose language and writing may still be hesitant but whose calligraphic standard in their first writing system might put other children to shame.

TAMIL WRITERS' DIFFICULTIES WITH 'O'

எண் பெயர் சசிபா

Circular letters in Tamil move in a clockwise direction. It looked, from their separate letters, as if the children had learned this lesson.

என் தந்தையின் பெயர்

I am in the Schoolroom..

என் பெயர் கேசவன்.

எ ன் தந்தையின் பெயர்

I am in the schoolroom.

Joining up double 'oo' showed them that there is still a long way to go.

room   rooom

room   room   room

room   roon   room

Tamil school children's problems with circular movements

A Tamil teacher in a small village school in Penang had worked out exercises to help his pupils alter the movement of circular letters from clockwise to anti clockwise. To him it was obvious where the difficulties lay – after all, he had had the same problems himself. However he had only dealt with separate letters and had not noticed how many children were masking the actual direction of circular movements in their neat print script. I tested his pupils by asking them all to join up the letters in the word 'room'. The exercise was greeted with some amusement but it soon showed that the changeover from one movement to another was far from easy. Exercises in a joined script made it obvious that more work was needed. The letter 'o' is likely to cause problems for them for some time to come.

A useful tip: incorrect movement may not be noticed in separate letters but becomes obvious when joined. When letters or characters look similar but move in the clockwise direction rather than anti clockwise there are likely to be problems, as circular movement are particularly hard to alter. Simple exercises should be devised to compare and contrast relevant letters, stressing the physical change as well as the visual one. If pupils find the results amusing, as they did here, all the better – they will have a good humoured reminder to be careful.

The pupil as a teacher

There is a more subtle purpose in asking children about their specific difficulties, especially if the question can be phrased in such a way that the pupil becomes the instructor. Not only does it force the writer to be analytical about his or her learning process, and help the teacher to understand on this and any future occasion, but it bestows on the learner the position of 'expert'. This can be instrumental in breaking down any barriers (real or imaginary) between teacher and pupil – and nothing can be more true. The writer is the real expert. The detailed explanations that many children perceived by their teachers as not particularly intelligent have given me, has helped towards an understanding of the subject that I could have arrived at in no other way.

Research

Research into the incidence of particular occurrences can help to
build the body of evidence needed to understand not only
individual problems but the deeper meaning of the act of writing
across cultural boundaries. The project reported in the next section
was prompted by a chance observation, yet somehow ended up
encompassing precisely the cross-cultural nuances that would be so
difficult to preordain. What at first seemed to be a colleague's
personal deviation turned out to be a fairly frequent consequence
of the strict training of making 'horizontal strokes before vertical
strokes' in Chinese characters. This colleague, a psychologist, said
what may well be true – the way that the Chinese sequence is the
best. This small project is unlikely to alter the way the letter 't' is
taught worldwide, but it may make people realise how much is to
be learned from studying those acquiring a second writing system.

I would like to reproduce the report exactly as it was published
in the proceedings of the conference where I presented it.
Inevitably the formality of the language differs from the rest of this
book. That is precisely what I would like to stress – and more.
The whole format of a research paper restricts issues to those that
can be 'proven', discounting the nuances and deeper intuitions that
might be just as valuable in certain circumstances. In *The Art and
Science of Handwriting* I tried to explain the struggle that I have had
reconciling the therapeutic and educational aspects of my work
with the demands of scientific research. In my multi-disciplinary
forays into handwriting there are marked differences in attitudes
between my scientific colleagues and my letterform ones, who
have been known to complain that I dwell in ridiculous detail on
subjects of little importance (such as the crossbar of the letter 't').

Far more frequently I have had my work criticised by scientific
colleagues as not scientific enough. The renowned artist, biologist
and anthropologist Jonathan Kingdon (with whom I was lucky to
work briefly in the department of fine art at Makerere in Uganda,
many years ago) puts this all into perspective saying: 'I find the
arbitrariness of personal experience a necessary antidote to the
impersonal categorisation which science tends to impose upon
nature. I am an enthusiastic scientist but I think that systems can
acquire an intellectual tyranny which usurps the authority of the
senses and can imprison the imagination' (from Kingdon, 1983).

The effects of an accustomed stroke sequence on the characters in a second writing system

This is an extended abstract of a paper that was presented at the fifth conference of International Graphonomics Society in Paris, (1993),

This study concentrates on the sequencing of the crossbar and downstroke in the letter 't'. It investigates the way that Chinese writers, trained in a specific stroke sequence in their first writing system (horizontal strokes before vertical) may consequently alter the conventional sequence of the strokes within certain characters in a second writing system. A consequence of this unconventional sequencing was first observed in the handwriting of a colleague in the Institute of Psychology during a visit to the Academia Sinica in Beijing. The psychologist in question found, as would be expected, that once his attention was drawn to this particular sequencing of strokes he was unable to replicate it in conscious writing. It seemed to occur only at a level of automatic writing. His comments are recorded and his letters are shown on p. 50.

Sequencing the letter 't' in a similar way to a Chinese character, the crossbar before the upright, can result in an unconventional appearance to the letter. This form of the letter had not been observed in a detailed analysis of the same letter (Sassoon, Wing and Nimmo-Smith, 1989). One related similarity, an isolated instance, was found in this analysis. It was produced by a left-hander who commenced the letter 't' with a right to left crossbar thus producing the characteristic triangular 'hat' found in the Chinese writer letterforms, but with the triangle to the left of the stem of the letter.

Several sets of work were collected from Chinese school children and university students to investigate the frequency of this occurrence. Samples of previously written work was used when writers could not be watched individually. In those cases the only instances that could be counted, even when the sequencing was probably the same, were when the pen was kept on the paper between strokes, resulting in the characteristic triangle on the 't's.

Method
A sequence of words was employed to obtain several examples of the letters 'th'. This consisted of a sentence starting with the words 'I think that the', and continued, in the guise of pen-preference questionnaire, in such a way as to hide the intent of the exercise. This questionnaire was allowed to be used with several groups of university students in Beijing. However it was not permitted to be

THE SEQUENCING OF CROSSBAR JOINS

National standardzation.

The first example that I had seen of this sequencing of the letter 't'.

I think that is

Asked to replicate it, the writer reverted to standard cursive forms.

t t l   t l (t)

He could not consciously reproduce that first unusual form of 't'.

most efficientq to write the 'way of

Chinese 'sequence.

He concluded that writing the Chinese way was more efficient for him.

I studi^{ed} English handwriting in 1959.
what I learned the style is like above

In 1964. we got the new English textbook.
and teacher asked & us to change our style of
English letter - writings. So two styles are confuse
each other. The latter style using, to write English
is unfamiliar but more quickly.

How this arose. In this case the simpler style of semi-cursive allowed writers more freedom and resulted in forms that are more natural for those trained in a horizontal-before-vertical stroke sequencing.

used in any school either in north or south China. It was possible to observe classes in action, and certain examples that had been produced in those classes were allowed to be retained for analysis. It could be said that this method satisfied the criterion of being spontaneous handwriting and it could be judged as fortuitous that the letter combination to be tested is perhaps the most commonly used in the English language.

The examples of high school pupils work consisted of a set of dictation papers which inevitably included several examples of the word 'the'. The younger children were given a short set of phrases by their teacher. It was possible to watch each of these twelve-year-old pupils in action and therefore to obtain an exact count of the sequencing of their strokes in the letters to be analysed.

Schematic illustrations of the join from the letter 't' to 'h'.

1 The conventional baseline join
2 One variation of the crossbar join
3 A left-hander's solution with a right to left horizontal stroke before vertical
4 The Chinese writers' solution with a left to right horizontal stroke before vertical and *below* how this relates to simple Chinese characters.

Results

A group of twelve-year-old pupils in Guanzhou provided an opportunity to observe the children in action and therefore to ascertain precisely how many children sequenced the horizontal stroke before the vertical. It was observed that six pupils out of the group of 24 did so (25%). In no case did the pupils allow their pens to rest on the paper between the two strokes so the characteristic 'hat' was not visible in their handwritten examples. This means that had it not been possible to view each writer in action there would have been no indication of their sequencing of the strokes of the letter 't'.

Out of 55 high school students aged 17–18 years old from a high school in Guanzhou (the same school as above):

19 (34.6%) showed horizontal before vertical sequencing in the letter 't' in the combination t-h at some stage in their dictation.
11 (20%) used a crossbar join at some stage, indicating that the vertical stroke was written first.
1 showed the characteristic 'hat' of horizontal stroke, in addition to a separate crossbar
1 used an idiosyncratic form and sequence of the letter resembling a Chinese character rather than a letter 't'.

EXAMPLES FROM THREE SETS OF WRITERS

I think that the best kind pen for me is ___ball-pen___,

because it helps me to write ___quickly and smoothly___

I think that the best rind of pen for me

Two examples from university students demonstrating the use of the crossbar before the down stroke of the letter 't'.

to climb the tall tree towards the enemy's

tall tree, as the had passed by with then

sitting in frant of it, to climb the tall tree as the

From among the high school pupils' work, from the top:

One student sequencing the crossbar before the down stroke.

One student using a conventional crossbar and one written before the down stroke.

One student forming the letter 't' as if it were a Chinese character

Come and look at the elephants.

Are there any lions and tigers in the zoo?

Younger pupils were being taught separate letters using an italic model. To detect their sequencing of 't' they had to be watched.

In 23 cases it was impossible to tell which stroke was written first.

Out of 84 university students in Beijing:

7 (8.33%) showed that they sequenced the horizontal before the vertical in the word 'the'.

14 (16.66%) demonstrated the use of the crossbar join in the word 'the' which showed that they sequenced the vertical stroke before the horizontal.

In 56 cases it was impossible to tell which stroke was written first.

The small group of pupils who were watched individually suggest how the use of previously written examples might distort the report of the frequency of this sequencing in the other groups analysed here. However there is another well-known factor that might have distorted these figures. When someone is being watched they are aware of this and often revert to a conscious mode of writing. This was demonstrated in the first case of the psychologist – when writing in conscious mode the writer is less likely to betray the very features that we were trying to tabulate.

Discussion

The Latin alphabet depends to a certain extent on the acceptance of the conventional stroke sequence if the resulting writing is to be recognisable, particularly at speed. However there is considerable latitude in some letters, especially in those that have distinctive characteristics – such as the letters 't', 'k' or 'f' or 's'. It is not the intention of this investigation to show the unusual sequencing of the letter 't' as a fault. Indeed it is an efficient and acceptably legible solution to sequencing a crossbar, in particular in the initial position in a word. It could be argued that this form of the letter might be taught to those whose first writing system had accustomed them to sequencing the horizontal before the vertical. The psychologist whose handwriting sparked off this survey said that it is 'Most efficient to write the way of Chinese sequences'.

However, even the simple analyses shown here demonstrate how much can be learned about the skill of handwriting from studies of those acquiring a second writing system. This study reinforces the large body of work that accentuates the effects of motor programming on the acquisition of the skill of handwriting. It raises other questions as well. In an educational context, informed

When my daughter was working in Japan learning the language and writing Kanji her letters betrayed the influence of the strict sequencing. She started to use the same strategy in English for separate letters and also when joining to the letter 't'. This habit stopped after she returned to Europe and no longer spoke or wrote in Japanese.

but common sense considerations are needed to ascertain where writers from different cultures might find problems in acquiring any particular writing system. This study has confined itself to the letterform aspects alone and to only one specific pair of letters. The analyses of the sequencing of capital and other cursive forms within these examples could provide a wealth of additional information of interest to educational and forensic studies.

Cross-cultural handwriting research.

In the specific circumstances mentioned, I found observation and questioning more useful than formal research. For other purposes research is vital, and very little cross-cultural work relevant to handwriting has been undertaken. I have searched in vain, for instance, for any information concerning hand development in different countries, even within Europe, where children start school at different ages. Some evidence suggests that they may develop different penholds and writing strategies as a result. If this were studied across cultures much more might be discovered. I myself have only glimpsed such developmental differences when observing and photographing young children's hands in multi-cultural play groups in various countries.

Joint projects, or independent but linked studies, in two or more countries simultaneously must be encouraged, however difficult and expensive they may be to set up.

A few issues that influence handwriting have been researched cross-culturally. Such studies provide techniques that can be replicated in other countries. Directionality and stroke sequencing are two such subjects, related inextricably to each other. Nihei (1983) describes his work in that field as searching for the universal principles or rules in drawing and handwriting which are called a 'grammar of action'. This had been researched across cultural boundaries, to a certain extent, by Lieblich and Ninio (1976) and Goodnow (1977). Two more recent works on directionality and stroke sequencing that have influenced my own views have been those of Lurçat (1985) in France and Nihei (1983) in Japan. Tests used in these researchers' various studies should transcend cultural barriers and provide useful data concerning the universal graphic development of children.

Those of us who are interested in using the written trace for research, or as a diagnostic aid, are often envious of the Chinese.

They have the advantage of being able to observe and measure many more factors through their complex characters than is possible within an alphabetic system. This might be when assessing brain damage, (Butterworth and Yin, 1991) typographic perceptions (Chuang and Cheng 1986), or spatial features in the context of deaf signing, (Fok and Bellugi (1986), (see pages 10, 23 and 131). Much of what is written about the writing systems of the world is done so either by those interested in the aesthetic/ calligraphic aspects or from the historic perspective. From some of these papers, written by neurologists, neuro-psychologists or psychologists, a different view of writing systems is presented – and one that has considerably extended my own knowledge.

No chapter such as this would be complete without mention of the work of Professor Henry Kao. His contributions vary from ergonomic studies of pen points and angles to the physiological changes that calligraphers undergo in the course of writing Chinese characters. It is appropriate that these words from Kao (1992) should end this chapter:

> It is virtually impossible to make one-for-one comparisons between and sometimes even within cultures. A knowledge of language or even of assimilation into a culture for a short period gives little rise to an ability to judge the nature of the underlying psychology and its relevance to another culture.
>
> Without a knowledge of the foundations unique to a culture it will be most unlikely that any unique attributes which are culturally bound can be found.... Even within a given culture it is naive to believe that all behaviors emerge from a singularly held belief within a culture. Thus to interpret a behavioral pattern as existing in some universally causal manner within or among cultures is surely inadequate.

Professor Kao was not necessarily referring to handwriting studies but what he says is relevant to the examples of cross-cultural problems illustrated in this chapter. Although a pattern of common problems might be expected between any two cultures or writing systems, individual perceptions and personal differences are always likely to upset any preconceived ideas. This section is only an introduction for those who work in this field to use as a framework for their own observations and to build on in the future.

THE USE OF THE HAND

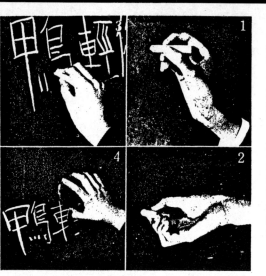

Teaching teachers to use chalk on the blackboard and details of pencil and brush hold from *Handwriting Exercises for Elementary Schools*, Hong Kong. The sub-title of this book is: *The Systematic Understanding and Thinking Behind the Teaching of Handwriting*. This emphasises how important the subject is considered to be and the illustrations show how detailed the instructions are for both teachers and children.

Left:
A Japanese schoolboy at work demonstrating how the arm and wrist are not supported while writing.

CHAPTER 4

Writing Materials and Writing Posture

Writing implements, along with whole writing systems, originally developed in their various and characteristic ways depending largely on what materials were freely available in the locality at the time. Implements varied from stick to reed to feather, or alternatively, to a primitive brush or stylus of a shape, size and sharpness that would be appropriate for whatever material it was to be used with. This might have been clay, papyrus, bone or perhaps palm leaves or bark. With time, other materials became available – wax and wooden tablets, metal plates, vellum, silk and, of course, paper. The influence of the original materials became embedded in the written forms, and sometimes, even now, when all materials are generally available worldwide, these influences are still felt. Some of the effects of the original (or early) writing implements have become so much part of the culture that modern influences may be felt as an intrusion, a betrayal of some part of the cultural heritage. Others are integral to the writing system and are so significant in the design of whole families of characters that they cannot easily be altered or simplified. Sometimes the direction of writing was also influenced by the tool.

The direction of writing is beginning to change in some cultures. There are systems, like Japanese, which are in transition. Newspapers may be set so that the characters are read from left to right along the line, whereas writers may still use the traditional layout of downward columns reading from right to left or, alternatively, lines that read from the same direction. Advertising logos behave in whatever way the designer likes, making things complicated for the unfortunate reader. In Chinese communities worldwide some of the same variations can be seen. As for the writing implement, in both Japan and China the brush is rapidly being overtaken by the ballpoint pen – but is enough thought given to any necessary alterations in writing posture, penhold or paper position that might be needed as a result of such changes?

ENGLISH AND HEBREW

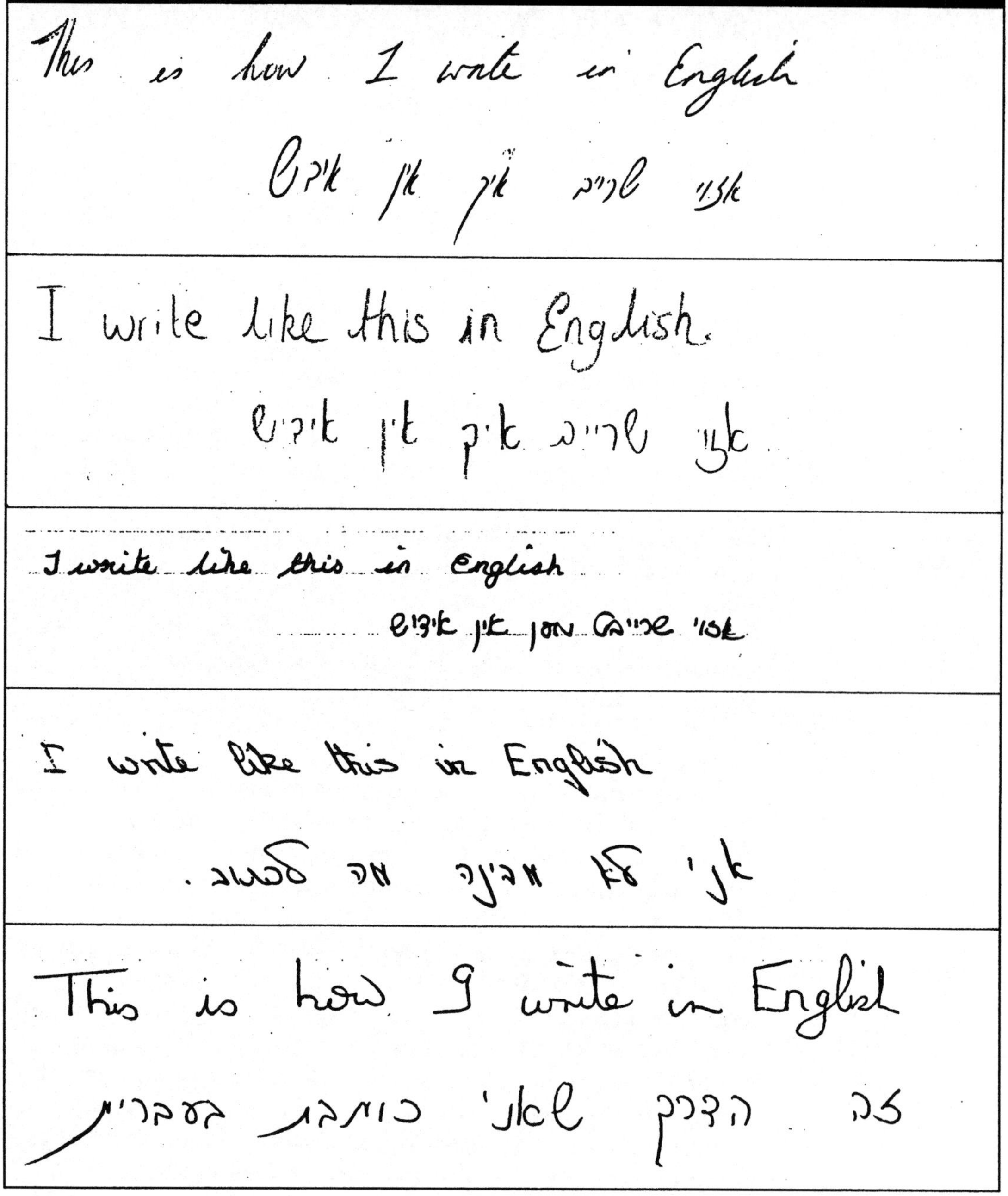

This is how I write in English

[Hebrew handwriting]

I write like this in English.

[Hebrew handwriting]

I write like this in English

[Hebrew handwriting]

I write like this in English

[Hebrew handwriting]

This is how I write in English

[Hebrew handwriting]

Opposite:
These teachers in a bi-lingual school were all given an exercise. It was to write alternately down a page: 'I write like this in English and I write like this in Hebrew.' Three wrote in Yiddish and two in Hebrew, with one writing: 'I do not understand what I am supposed to do' instead of the correct wording.

This all makes an exact comparison of characters difficult, but even a cursory glance shows similarities in the slant and proportion of letters in each set. The last example was produced by the only writer to alter her hand position when changing the direction of her writing. In the top example the hand position seemed to inhibit the formation of some Hebrew letters especially the aleph.

Aleph from top writer.

Aleph from last writer

This chapter looks first at some of the practical problems which writers learning a second writing system may experience as a result of alterations in the direction of the writing across the page. Alterations in writing posture as a result of change either in direction or of writing implement are also dealt with. Difficulties that are encountered may depend on whether the two writing systems are being learned simultaneously or whether the second one is being assimilated after a lengthy period during which the writing posture of the first one will have become automated.

Direction

It is surprising how few pupils report serious difficulties over directionality. Those who do are, in my experience, mostly those for whom directionality is a problem anyhow – and these are not uncommon in any classroom. Few adults who have learned Hebrew or Arabic first and English afterwards report that they have experienced difficulties, but those who do say that their problems have not improved with time. They complain that they still get confused when they stop in mid-sentence or even mid-word. The momentum of fast writing can often help the writer who is confused to carry on in the desired direction. It is a break in concentration, or an insistence on slow neat handwriting, that can cause problems. The understandable hesitation that may occur when learning to write in a second language might also add to any directional confusion.

In schools in England I sometimes get conflicting evidence – teachers may report that their pupils have little problem with directionality in the classroom, but sometimes the children tell me that it is with their Arabic in religious classes that their problems arise. Perhaps when a second writing system is being learned after the first but without enough time for the first to be automatic then it is like two languages – they get confused. When two languages are being learned simultaneously from the beginning, as with bilingual children whose parents use two different languages with them in the home from babyhood, it seems easier to deal with. It is always possibile that the teachers of one or the other writing systems are not aware of the importance of dealing with directional problems. Nothing can be taken for granted.

ENGLISH AND ARABIC

This · is English

اِبِن جاوي

This is English

اِن جاوي

This is English

اِبِن جاوی

This is English

ابن جاوي

These Arabic writers were given the same exercise as the teachers on the previous page. The most noticeable feature is how the slant of the two alphabets remains constant within each handwriting. None of these teachers altered their hand position between sentences, and all confessed to discomfort when writing in both alphabets, perhaps as a result of assuming a compromise over their hand position.

Hand and paper position

Alterations to both hand position and paper position are likely to be needed when dealing with two scripts that work in different directions. With a script that moves from left to right, it is usually best for the writer to place the paper to the side of the hand that writes and to slant it a little if it is more comfortable that way. With the paper to the side the writer can see what is being written as the hand progresses across the page. It is only fairly recently that this advice has been given in handwriting manuals even in England. In old-fashioned books a central paper position was recommended, reflecting the fact that few left-handers were allowed to write with their preferred hand, and it is left-handers who benefit most from having the paper to the side of the hand that writes. A 'sit up straight, put your paper straight in front of you' attitude prevailed in the days when speed was not essential. The comfort of writers was seldom taken into consideration. Left-handers whose hand obscures what has just been written, and often smudges it too, may resort to a hooked (inverted) hand position unless they are taught to place the paper over to their left side.

This boy reported that he had no trouble writing in English at school but difficulty with the direction of Arabic in his religious classes.

In other writing systems different rules concerning paper position are obviously needed. Chinese and Japanese children are usually taught to place the paper centrally and straight. This was necessary for the manipulation of the brush, and occurred in systems where left-handedness was not accepted. In addition, the detail within a character means that the movement of writing (and therefore the hand) downwards or across the line is not as pronounced as in an alphabetic script, particularly a cursive one.

In Arabic, where a cursive form of writing moves fast along the line from right to left, a different paper position is to be expected. From pictures of traditional Arabic scribes, always writing with their right hand, it can be seen that they used to rest their writing material on their right knee, so it was automatically to their right side. I do not want to be prescriptive here, in an area where I have little personal experience. However, I would just like to draw attention to the possible plight of a student coming to Arabic or Chinese when he or she was already established as a left-hander and unable to write well with a right hand.

Paper position becomes automated just like any other aspect of handwriting, and the student cannot be expected to realise that an alteration in paper position might be desirable. Teachers should be on the lookout for pupils who adopt an awkward writing posture when moving from any writing system to another. The position of the paper affects the position of the hand and sometimes the whole body. Students deserve an informed explanation.

A project in Malaysia looked into this problem. Four scripts (Arabic, Latin, Chinese and Tamil) and five languages are dealt with in a well-organised educational system, divided into three sections – Malay, Chinese and Tamil – to deal with the three main language groups. I was asked to visit schools with the brief of looking for handwriting problems. With a detailed and well thought out national handwriting policy, which taught handwriting through a systematic method that did not impose a model, it seemed at first that there were no discernable difficulties. It was only when visiting Malay schools where it had recently become compulsory for some lessons to be taught in Jawi, (Arabic with a few Malaysian variations), that something interesting arose. I had long been interested in the hand positions of those writing from right to left, hoping that this might hold some clues to help left handers in a left to right writing system.

The calligrapher at work, sitting on the ground with his right knee drawn up to support the paper. From a 16th century Turkish manuscript (Safadi 1978).

A colleague, Gregory James, who had spent many years in Iran teaching English to Farsi writers, told me how he had used an ingenious method of videoing his students at their most awkward stage, at the beginning their English course. After he had shown them how to adjust their paper and hand position to be more suited to the opposite direction of writing, he took more pictures to stress this important point.

I wanted to see this for myself, so being without any sophisticated equipment, set both teachers and pupils a simple task, on a small sheet of paper. Everyone was asked to write the sentence 'I write like this in English' alternated with the sentence 'I write like this in Jawi'. To my amazement, none of the adults or children altered either their hand position or paper when they altered from a left-to-right script to a right-to left one. They all seemed to have found a compromise position that seemed to work adequately for both systems. When I asked if they were comfortable like that, many of them admitted that they found writing awkward if not painful in both alphabets. They found the concept of different positions novel but comfortable. That particular situation was a consequence of a recent political decision that made teachers teach and write secular lessons in Jawi. Until then school lessons had been in English and Bahasa Malay, which also uses the Latin alphabet. The religious teachers would probably have been more knowledgeable even though most of their instruction would have been oral.

The use of the left hand

I learned much more on that trip – and some of it was in Chinese schools. When visiting mainland China I had accepted without question what I was told: that using the left hand was undesirable. This made sense to me, as I realised that the left to right direction of all horizontal strokes was essential to the ductus of characters and that this often posed problems for left-handers. In a class of young Chinese children in Kuala Lumpur, a teacher asked me to help with a left-hander who was having trouble forming his characters correctly. I explained the likely cause, only to be shown two other left-handers in the same room who were managing to write their characters perfectly happily. This school allowed children to write with whichever hand they wanted, and this teacher had not previously found it a problem. The child with difficulties was encouraged to switch to his right hand with the assistance of a 'magic' plastic pen grip. What the future held for him was uncertain, but he showed better control with his right hand straight away. So traditional rules are breaking down. This may help some left-handers but hinder others. Those with a strong right to left directionality may always have problems.

Penhold

As more and more countries forsake traditional implements and take to the ballpoint, they may discover the problems of penhold that plague this generation of writers in the Western world. Unconventional penholds abound. Some work well for individual writers, but upset the more traditional teachers who try, usually without effect, to make their pupils alter them. My own research, reported in the companion to this volume, *The Art and Science of Handwriting*, points to the need to reassess our attitude to penhold. We should be considering the use of a different penhold with modern pens, which work at a different elevation from traditional fountain pens or pencils. I took this idea to China and tried out the alternative penhold that I recommend for use with modern pens, in different circumstances. The most distorted and potentially painful-looking set of hands was to be found in a secretarial college in Hong Kong where the students were learning speedwriting. All the students changed to the alternative penhold as an experiment and all professed to finding relief from pain. I would like to think that some of them persisted in using the new penhold. The look of incredulity, followed by outright disapproval on the tutor's face, made me think that they would find little encouragement there.

At a slightly more academic level, I put the same suggestion to a set of university students in mainland China. The answer was interesting. After persisting for a while, the majority agreed that the alternative penhold, as used with the inexpensive ballpoint that they all had, was an improvement and voted it a great success when writing in English. Many of the students reported, however, that they found that they did not have enough control when writing Chinese characters with that penhold. I can suggest several reasons for this, but feel strongly that it is only by such surveys that we can find the answers to the many questions that need answering today.

I had to consider all these issues when explaining the problems in a book for parents of mainly Chinese children, who were learning English. A few points may be repeated from previous sections, but the text is presented here in its original form.

Practical matters that may have to be altered
You need to think first of all what alterations your child will need to make in the way he or she works, but first of all it is important that the child is seated comfortably. The height of the desk and the suitability of the chair can make all the difference between relaxed writers and those who suffer discomfort when they have to do a lot of writing. Then the issues concerning the alteration in writing system must be understood:

1 Should the writer necessarily use the same hand as he or she used before? Chinese teachers may have considered it best not to permit children to use their left hand when learning to sequence their characters, but with the alphabet it is not such

a problem. Quite a few children find it easier to write with their left hand, so it may be advisable to let children use the hand that they find best when they write in English.

2 Does the writer need to put the paper in a different place? When you write you need to see what you have just written and also be able to move your hand and arm easily as you progress along the page. The position of the paper may have to be changed when you learn a new writing system. When writing in an alphabet that goes from left to right it is best for right-handers to put their paper slightly over to their right side, then it can be tilted a little if the writer likes. Left-handers need their paper over to their left side, so they can see what they have just written. They may also like to tilt the paper slightly. This idea of moving the paper may seem strange to those who have always thought that paper should be placed straight in front of the writer, but this is important for young children. Wrongly placed paper is one of the main reasons for children sitting awkwardly. Once anyone gets used to any habit that affects the body it becomes increasingly difficult to alter, so it is important to get these matters sorted out at the start. The size of the paper needs thinking about too. If it is too large, a small child will have trouble writing at the top of the sheet.

3 Do the writers need to alter the way they hold the pen, or even the pen or pencil that they used before? The letters need to flow easily along the page so, particularly at the beginning, a child needs a pen or pencil that flows easily. A soft-leaded pencil may need to be sharpened more often than a hard one, but it will be better for a beginner because it will not dig into the paper. At the next stage a fibre-tipped point will probably be better than a ballpoint because it is more flexible. These small points all add up to make the task of learning to write the alphabet easier.

It is not easy to be exact about penhold. The conventional way is with the pen between the thumb and first finger, resting on the middle finger. Young children's hands are not all the same, however, so there will be slight differences in their penholds, and modern pens mean that there are variations in the angle that pens have to be held. The important thing is for each child to be able to produce the strokes that make up the letters in a relaxed way with whatever they are writing with.

A list for left-handers

The Latin alphabet undoubtedly works better for right-handers, but if your child is naturally left-handed then it is usually best for him or her to use the left hand to write in English. Here are a few hints to make things easier for left-handers:

1 Find a chair that is high enough, perhaps a little higher than you would use for a right-hander. This helps children to see what they are writing without having to twist their hand out of the way.

2 Use a softish pointed pen or pencil that does not dig into the paper and hold it far enough up the handle so the writer can see what he or she is writing.

3 Place the paper over to the left side, slanting it slightly if desired. This allows writers to move their arm freely, to see what has just been written, and still keep their hand below the line of writing.

4 Left-handers may find it harder to get used to proceeding from left-to-right along the page. A reminder of where to start, such as a red line down the side of the page, may help in the early stages. If a child shows signs of 'mirror writing', where letters face in the wrong direction, that is another sign that a left-hander needs a little more help in remembering the direction of forming strokes, letters or even whole words .

Left-handers who are expected to follow a strict model may have a problem with the slant of their letters. A slightly backward slant is often the easiest for them, and providing this is not so great as to affect legibility, this should not cause any problem (other than in the mind of some teachers). In addition, left-handers may profit from more penlifts when they get to the stage of joined writing. Some joins can be particularly awkward and the writing will flow better without them. If teachers would try to demonstrate to left-handers with their left hands it would not only help the children, but it would also help teachers to appreciate their pupils' problems.

The history and use of traditional materials

Before the subject of tools and materials is completed I would like to introduce the idea that the study of traditional tools and materials in any or all writing systems is not only of great interest to children and adults alike, but can lead to some imaginative techniques when dealing with reluctant writers.

My own work in this field has been limited to courses on the history of writing and tool-making in school. This is reported in Sassoon and Lovett (1992). It is my belief that such work would be invaluable in classrooms of children from different cultural backgrounds, giving an understanding of, and pride in the different writing systems. But there is more to it than that. Traditional tools are not to be scorned. A home-made pen, in whatever form, stick, feather, reed or bamboo, may capture the imagination of a reluctant writer and lead to a more relaxed attitude to writing. This could be followed up by the preparation (or at least a discussion) of different kinds of material to write on, and the grinding up of the different ingredients that might be used for making ink in various parts of the world. In a more adult environment, experiments with the tool most suited to the writing system can lead to an understanding of the forms and ductus of a writing system.

APPROPRIATE TESTS FOR DIFFERENT CULTURES

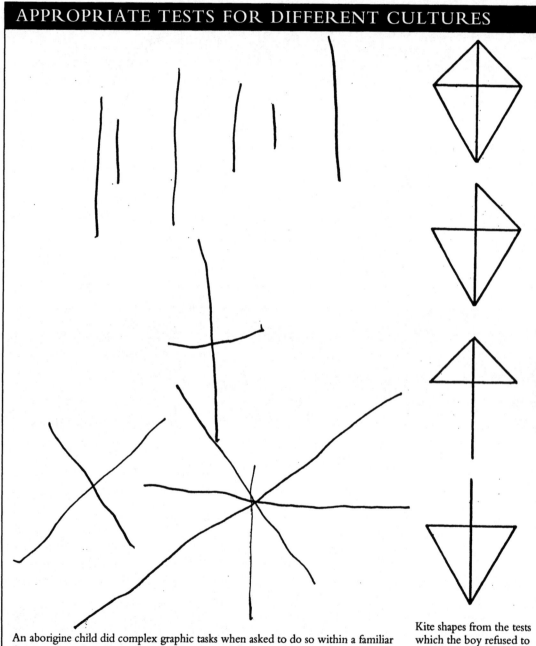

An aborigine child did complex graphic tasks when asked to do so within a familiar framework – when illustrating a story – but refused to cooperate with a formal test.

Kite shapes from the tests which the boy refused to complete (see p. 74).

CHAPTER 5

Assessment

Handwriting itself is an indicator of any writer's condition and as such is a useful diagnostic aid. It reacts with other cognitive skills and this needs to be borne in mind when making assessments of anyone writing in another writing system or even another language. However well taught the second writing system may be, language limitations and inhibition may show through the handwriting as lack of fluency. To get a fair picture of a pupil's innate abilities, some evidence in a writer's first writing system (and/or language) is advisable to compare with the writing in the second one. This helps to avoid judgements that might be made from the visual effects of hesitation in the learner's handwriting.

With beginners, any assessment of writing skill might be better if it did not include words – just letter patterns. Any thorough assessment of progress should, where possible, include written work both in the writer's first language and writing system – even when an interpreter might be needed to assess content. This is yet another area where it is not possible to separate language from the act of writing.

The way that language problems intervene in handwriting was clearly demonstrated to me a short while ago by the case of a young trainee teacher in a bilingual community and educational system. Her first alphabet was written from right to left. She reported that she seldom wrote a word in English without having to correct it and her tutors were worried about the effects of her poor handwriting on her examination results. At first we wondered if some of her difficulties with writing in English stemmed from being left-handed and having directional problems. As we talked, however, I became aware of deficiencies in her spoken English. Her story gradually unfolded. She had not spoken English until emigrating to America at the age of eight or nine. Then she had always spoken her first language at home, so had a relatively limited vocabulary, which was sprinkled with Americanisms that allowed her to communicate orally but covered up her inadequate knowledge of grammar. Her tutors were pressing for handwriting exercises when what she needed was a grounding in the language

COMPARING CONTENT IN TWO WRITING SYSTEMS

3. she sit the chair, chair broken.

4 she looking thee Porridge No hot gololi locks eat Porridge ena.

5. she look three bed, she sleeping baby bed.

这个小姑娘她吃完以后的燕团,
于是就想找一猴来睡一下. 她来到卧室
发现里面有三张床, 二张大床一张小床. 她先
第一张床, 太硬, 第二张床太长了. 她最后
上第三张床. 不大不小, 刚刚而且很软, 她
很快就进入了梦乡绍

Translation:
After this little girl finished her rice, she felt tired so she wanted to find a bed to sleep. She went to the bedroom, she saw three beds, two big ones and one small bed. She climbed on the first bed, it was too hard. The second bed was too long. At last she climbed on the third bed which was not so big, and not so small, it was just right and very soft. She fell asleep immediately.

A Chinese child attempted an exercise consisting of a sequence of six pictures illustrating the story of Goldilocks. She had to write about each picture in English and Chinese. Her English was limited. The one paragraph in Chinese that space permits gives an idea of her real intellectual level and demonstrates how wrong it is to judge children by their performance in a second language or writing system.

CONTENT AND HANDWRITING IN TWO LANGUAGES

Jon said
Mother, hau we are going to
park
In the, park is very good,
but Jon silly boy said.
hot hot. but his mother is
camin and to give him some
water

Rata creață și-ndrăsneață

A fost odată ca niciodată un moș și o babă
Aăsti bătrâni aveau o rață care era tare în-
drăsneață
Into o bană oi anastă rală a căzut cu laba into-
ballă Atunci lina, boa se duce la babă oîndu-
cal să i stearaă laba. Atunci babo î-asis să
nu a mai pomenit o asemenea rață cași
ă ceară stălime să ii stearaă laba Otunei

Translation: The Curly Daring Duck
Once upon a time there was an old man and an old woman.
These two old folk had a duck which was very daring. One
day this duck soiled one of its flippers in a pond. And then,
splash, splash, it went to the old woman and asked her to
wipe it off. Then the old woman told the duck that she had
never heard of a duck asking her mistress to wipe its flippers
off... and so on for a whole page without any spelling
mistakes.

From the handwriting of this 'New Australian' you
might get the impression of a rather immature child.
The handwriting in his first language demonstrates his
maturity, even before the translation shows the quality
of the content of his work.

before anything else. No wonder her handwriting was hesitant. Without the vocabulary or grammar to construct a sentence handwriting exercises are useless.

This problem is put into a theoretical form by Peer (1991) in a short article entitled *Bilingualism and dyslexia*. She reports that 'In bilingual children the language sample available in the home and school is different from that experienced by monolingual children, and this will significantly affect their understanding of the essential structure of language, particularly in cases where the student has short term memory inefficiencies.... The bilingual student has two vocabularies, two rule systems, two structures, giving a multiplicity of verbal labels for the idea. This makes his representative language overly complex, and much less efficient than it should be.'

Peer is discussing bilingual children, which suggests that the student might be equally proficient in two languages. In the case stated earlier – and in many other cases – this is not so. The second language is often inadequately learned, and, according to what I am told by such students, most information is translated into the first language and then back again before it is written down.

Stress
Some problems are common to all writers. Tension, boredom, pain, fright all leave their marks on the written trace. Some of these signs are more likely to be evident in those whose traumatic experiences have led to their being refugees in another country, for instance. To add to their stress they may be confronted with an unfamiliar and sometimes hostile educational environment. The need to acquire a second writing system, as fast as possible, may exacerbate such problems, and not only in the most obvious way. Your handwriting is yourself on paper, the way you present yourself to the world. Your name writing and signature are even more a sign of you yourself. Imagination is needed to judge how much an alteration in self expression might affect a vulnerable pupil. I know of no research that has tackled this kind of problem.

A certain proportion of all writers may suffer from perceptual or motor problems. These might best be identified by looking at examples of a student's first writing system. Any page will usually provide some evidence to an informed eye, even when the language or writing system is unfamiliar.

Here is an example that illustrates this point. Before looking at examples of handwriting problems in Hong Kong, a teacher gave me her criteria for judging the Chinese characters written by the children with whom she dealt. These criteria were as follows:

Things added
Things left out
Wrong axis
Wrong placement
Reversal
Mirror image

My knowledge of Chinese characters is minimal, so many of these criteria were of no use to me and I was thrown back onto different judgements. I looked for inconsistencies, much as I would do in the case of an English-speaking child. This was made easier because all children, whatever their problems, were being asked to produce a whole sheet of the same character. Certain judgements could be made without being able to read the characters. For example, if in the case of an English child some letters or words stood out as well-written in a sea of badly written letters, then I would want to know what sort of tensions could be distorting a writer who was sometimes able to perceive or produce perfectly adequate letters and sometimes not. The same concept worked in Hong Kong where, to the surprise of the on-lookers (and to my own relief) it could be shown that some children started their task tensely but relaxed towards the middle of the page only to relapse towards the end of what could be termed an onerous and even boring task. My own belief is that if a child is able to write a perfect character at some stage then this should be possible all or most of the time in relaxed circumstances. Other judgements can sometimes be made by comparing the work of writers within a group. It is only when problems are evident all the time, and when they are markedly more evident in certain individuals than in the writing of their peers, that one can say a child cannot write properly. Even then it is a good idea to watch the child in action before attempting a detailed diagnosis.

While on the subject of writers in Hong Kong, it seemed to me that first of all the level of problems in such a complex task were minimal. Then the reported incidence appeared to be extremely low compared with the incidence in England. I can only conclude that the advantages of an early start on what has been traditionally acknowledged as a difficult task, allied to a systematic method, allows those who might otherwise have had problems, to develop their hand/eye coordination and control within that systematic method. The expectations are also traditionally much higher. This is certainly a lesson for educationists in the West to note.

Criteria and materials for testing

There is a need for more culturally appropriate assessment tests. The following examples show that where cultural inhibitions intervene, we may not get a clear picture of any child's capabilities. In a small Australian town I saw a young aboriginal boy of about six years old. He had been placed in a group of children with severe mental and physical problems – yet he appeared alert and was interesting to talk to. The tasks that all these children had been set on that particular day were:

1   To complete the first page of the Frostig assessment test, which consists of completing segments of a kite-like object.
2   To cut up three drinking straws and thread them onto a cord.

This little boy had previously refused to attempt this test, therefore he had been classified at the lowest possible level. He showed no interest in this task again with us (I was with a locum therapist that day). I had been told that aboriginal children learn best with a narrative approach, so I asked if I might experiment with some other tests based around the story that he kept telling us about a big snake that his father had killed.

First he was asked if he could draw a line of trees, some tall and some short – which he did quite happily – then the tracks of two kangaroos if they crossed in the sand, and finally the tracks of two more kangaroos if they intersected to form a six-sided star. He drew all this with no hesitation. These particular directional strokes are known to be a reliable indicator of graphic development, considerably more advanced than completing the sides of the kite. He had cooperated and shown a more realistic level of graphic development quite happily because the 'test' had been put in a more sensitive and interesting way for him. The motor test was even more startling. The therapist had brought along a whole collection of scissors and the child handled them all carefully before selecting one. He then lined up the three straws in an efficient manner and cut through them simultaneously, in a competent way, before threading them with no trouble at all. Yet this child had been classified as educationally subnormal, motorically incompetent and was doomed to be left in this inappropriate group. I was told that nothing could be done to persuade the authorities to alter this assessment.

The need for appropriate tests

If European or American assessments are used in inappropriate circumstances, then cultural inhibitions, or lack of what might be thought of as everyday experience, can easily distort any test results. An Australian special needs teacher gave me a good example of this. An aboriginal child was being tested with a computer program which provided phrases and illustrations describing the making of a cup of tea. (She assured me that the child related quite happily to the computer.)The pupil was supposed to arrange the pictures and phrases into a logical sequence. He would be judged by the speed and accuracy of his sequencing. This task appeared to baffle the child until the teacher became aware that it was the electric kettle that was causing trouble. On questioning it appeared that the child was used to a pot of water on the fire, and although it was pointed out to him that there was an electric kettle in the classroom, it became clear that he had not related to it other than as just another inexplicable artifact. Once it was all explained there were no further problems, and as the teacher related, it was a learning experience for both the people involved.

These are just two cases to illustrate, in extreme circumstances, the consequences of cultural inhibition, but there are wider implications for other testing. When you consider the somewhat minimal tasks that Western children are given to test for motor delay, think how inadequate they might be for communities where children, from an early age, have been trained to balance a water pot on their heads. Think how culturally inappropriate some sight tests are, or maybe even tests for colour vision, for those whose concept of colours (bright or dark for instance) are different from the testers'. There are dangers for countries with newly emerging special needs departments who might follow American or British testing methods. Those devising ones more appropriate for their own children should be given every encouragement.

Remediation techniques

For remediation, a system that is familiar may work best in what is often a tense situation. If the pupil is familiar with characters in squares, as many Chinese and Japanese children are, then use squares – if a formal copybook system is familiar then use that, even if that system might be frowned upon as too formal in the mainstream classroom. Some children may be missing the comfort of formality in an unfamiliarly progressive atmosphere. For those who may prove unable to progress in new surroundings, then use whatever is culturally acceptable – a stick in sand, a brush and paint, even coloured sand dribbled through the hand, to teach movement and provide motivation to communicate.

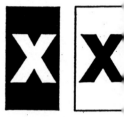

Illustrations from Sassoon (1991) Linguaphone Children's English.

This discussion of appropriateness brings to mind an international refugee relief meeting when aid workers, based in camps in Vietnam and Cambodia, reported that they were unable to proceed with elementary educational services. They complained that this was because the *tape recorders and not even the blackboards or pens* had arrived. The suggestion that the large cardboard food cartons could be utilised, with home-made charcoal from the fire, if necessary, was greeted with horror. Evidently illiteracy was preferable to asking a 'teacher' to work without sophisticated but not necessarily appropriate equipment.

Criticism

How to judge an individual's progress in handwriting, or in the content of written work, is difficult enough in ordinary circumstances. What criteria to use and how to encourage a necessary level of self-criticism without discouraging the writer when involved with a second writing system and language is more complex still. It needs sensitive handling.

With young children, the school's attitude to the use of their first language, much less their writing system is formative. For a child in a new school in a new country there is a careful balance between the need to communicate in a second language and the retention of and pride in their first. While instruction may need to be in the second language, it is likely to be difficult for the pupil with a limited vocabulary (or command of the writing system) to communicate fully. In addition to the practical problems, he or she may have a fear of criticism or ridicule. Different attitudes are to be found. I liked this liberal comment from West Australia. Alison Dewsbury, from the Curriculum Development Branch of the Ministry of Education, described a project in a local school with a high proportion of 'New Australians'. Teachers encourage the beginners to use both languages interchangeably, switching codes as they please. Progress is fast. The teachers allow the children to use their own language when they are stuck. If the teacher does not understand it does not matter as long as the children understand each other – as long as they communicate.

When it comes to a second writing system it can be harder to make such decisions. Not long ago I visited an interesting school in North London attended by children of 26 nationalities. A young boy from Ethiopia was in the classroom, being given one-to-one teaching to accelerate his language learning. I was told that he either did not know, or had forgotten, how to write Amharic. When he was shown some examples of Amharic typefaces, which I happened to have with that day, he became quite excited and immediately began explaining how the accents worked in his own writing system. When I left a few minutes later, he was teaching his (Somali) teacher how to write in Amharic. I caught up with him a little later in a language class. He was in a group of six children comprising five different nationalities. All these children were being invited to translate various key words (witch and crocodile among them) in the story that they were reading into their own language, for their satisfaction and the interest of the class. I only wish that such attention were paid to the children's first writing systems. Many of these children were refugees from war zones. It is to be hoped that they will return to their homes sometime in the future, and their skills may be needed to rebuild the economies of their countries. If they no longer write their first alphabet, however much official paperwork may be carried out in English, their usefulness will be limited.

DIFFERENCES IN GRAPHIC ABILITY

1) என் பெயர் கோகிலவாணி

2) என் தந்தையின் பெயர் திரு கண்ணையா

1) I am in the schoolroom.

2) My name is Kokilavani ॥

Pupils' problems are likely to show through their handwriting, These two Tamil pupils, from the same class, demonstrate two different levels of ability. This shows clearly in both their first and second scripts, and even in their numerals. With poor control when writing in Tamil the handwriting of the pupil whose work is shown below would inevitably reflect the same problems when he was writing in English.

1 என் பெயர் சுந்தரேசன்

2 என் தந்தையின் பெயர் திருப்பதம்.

1 I am in the school room.

2 My name is Sundaresan

Older students

A balance is needed not only between learning a new writing
system and preserving the first one, but in criticism and
encouragement at all times. Anne Wortham, who teaches high
achieving second language students in Australia, has definite views
on the effects of criticism. She says that she experiences difficulty
in convincing students from Chinese cultures, in particular, how
much they have absorbed and how well they have absorbed it. She
explains that this is because classroom teachers tend to correct
work by looking for errors and making them obvious. To second
language students such criticism can diminish what they have
already absorbed and can destroy it, making the task even more
difficult, even futile. She explains how depressed students become,
losing a sense of what there is to be learned because no one is ever
satisfied with what they have done. She quotes a high level student
from Taiwan who said that he still felt illiterate (quite
undeservedly) after three years because of constant criticism. Her
suggestions are reassuring: 'Always when we correct we should
express delight at how well *something* has been accomplished.
Narrow the goals, transmitting a specific but limited bit of
information, say a ten minute exercise, that can be absorbed and
tested reassuringly at the next session. If handwriting is bad, praise
spelling, if grammar appals then praise organisation.'

Anne Wortham has a sensitive insight into the minds of her
students, talking about the confusion and diminished sense of who
they are in an alien culture. Her students, as do so many others in
education, have a desperate need for someone to understand their
plight. She finds that when she tells them what she has told me
(and I have reported here), there is a great sense of relief that
someone understands, not only their present practical problems but
their high expectations and, more than that, the reality that they
are often the vehicles of other peoples' expectations and ambitions.

As I listened to Anne Wortham I felt even more strongly how
important it is that teachers should themselves have been in the
same position: to have experienced at first hand the baffling
confusion of learning another language and writing system, and to
have been unable to communicate orally or on paper at their own
intellectual level. Perhaps it is too much to ask that they should
also have been judged and criticised for their own inadequacies.

EXTENDED ALPHABETS

Yr Wyddor (the alphabet) from Phillips (1962) ABC y Plant. Trydydd Argraffiad. This set of letters includes the common letter combinations used specifically in the Welsh language

A	B	C	CH	D	DD
a	b	c	ch	d	dd
E	F	FF	G	NG	H
e	f	ff	g	ng	h
I	J	L	LL	M	N
i	j	l	ll	m	n
O	P	PH	R	RH	S
o	p	ph	r	rh	s
T	TH	U	W	Y	
t	th	u	w	y	

From *A maci ir*, a copybook for Hungarian schools by Virágvölgyi (1978). This set of letters includes those with accents and the specific combinations of letters used in the Hungarian language.

CHAPTER 6

Handwriting Models and Teaching Techniques

So far, the emphasis has been on the differences between writing systems, ignoring most of the linguistic problems and also the stylistic ones. In many fields it is known that altering a minor detail may be more difficult than adapting to something manifestly different. In literacy skills this might apply to the letter/sound relationship, or to the retraining of a motor movement in order to reproduce a letter. Any hesitation may affect the fluency of handwriting. Then take the problems of reading for Greeks learning English, for whom some familiar shapes suddenly represent a different sound. I can testify to how easy it is to miss a bus because you cannot work out its destination fast enough – even when you think that you are a fairly competent reader of Greek capital letters. I know a special-needs teacher who uses a block of text printed in Greek capitals to illustrate to parents of dyslexic children what a page of print might seem to them – something fairly familiar but inexplicably indecipherable.

Sets of letters

It has already been mentioned that an alphabet is often incapable of representing the sounds of a language which is manifestly different from the one for which it was developed – although there are various conventions that allow it to indicate them. The idea that there are 26 letters in the Latin alphabet is so deeply embedded in most English-speaking people's thoughts that they may find it surprising to find that there are other ways of presenting the alphabet to the learner. To take just two examples: Welsh, a Celtic language, and Hungarian, a Magyar language. In schools where Welsh is taught and in Hungarian schools, extended sets of letters are presented to the children. These sets of letters include those that are accented and particular letter combinations necessary to represent the characteristic sounds of the language e.g., 'll' and 'dd' in Welsh and 'cs', 'sz' and 'zs' in Hungarian.

DEVANAGARI

(i) vowels

অ আ ই ঈ উ ঊ ঋ এ ঐ ও ঔ

aw aa i ee u oo ri ay oi o ou

The Devanagari alphabet explained and separated into vowels, a consonant grid and diacritical marks by Trilokesh Mukherjee. He also gives some examples of joint letters and pairs to show the difference between typographic and written forms.

(ii) Consonents

according to different organs of articulation eg. palatar, labial etc.

ক ka	খ kha	গ ga	ঘ gha	ঙ unga
চ cha	ছ chha	জ ja	ঝ jha	ঞ iuga
soft ট ta	ঠ tha	ড da	ঢ dha	ণ na
hard ত ta	থ tha	দ da	ধ dha	ন na
প pa	ফ pha	ব ba	ভ bha	ম ma
শ sa	ষ sha	স ssa	ৎ t	
য ya	র 'ra	ল la	ৱ uwa	২ ha
ং ng	ঃ h	ঁ nasal		

(iii) diacritical marks

vowels

আ ই ঈ উ ঊ ঋ এ ঐ ও ঔ
বা বি বী বু বূ বৃ বে বৈ বো বৌ

consonents (samples)

ক্ষ র ফ য শ etc
র র র র র

ব্ + প + র + এ : ম্প্রায়
m + p + r + ay = mpray

(iv) on all four sides of a letter

ন্দ্রাঃ
ন্দ্রাঃ

ক + ষ = ক্ষ
K + sha = ksha

(v) joint letters

ন্ + প = ন্প
l + p = lp

প + ল = প্ল
p + l = pl

(vi) জ্ঞ = ক্ষ
type : written

ক্ত = ক্ত
type : written

iltuyj

hnmr

bpk

cadgqoe

vwxz sf

Letters presented in stroke related families: in a typeface (Sassoon Primary) that reflects the shape of written letterforms.

Alphabetical order

The order of the letters in the Latin alphabet presents learners with a particular problem as it appears to have no particular reason behind it. The letters, when in alphabetical order today, are not in groups that separate vowels from consonants, nor have they any relation to groups of sounds or to groups of related shapes or strokes. The reasons behind this seemingly illogical sequence are ancient in the extreme, according to Naveh (1975). He describes how: 'The West Semitic alphabetic order appears in the 14th century BC (in Ugarit) and was later adopted with a few changes in Greek and Latin, but the Arabic alphabetical order is different.'

Driver (1948) goes into the origin of alphabetical order much more thoroughly, saying that the order of the Phoenician alphabet is attested by the evidence of the Hebrew scriptures and that the Greek alphabet shows substantially the same order as the Hebrew. He reports that the most fantastic reasons for the order of letters have been suggested based, for example, on astral or lunar theories, He suggests another method based on seeking mnemonic words which may have been the basis of an alphabetic order. Some such words can be found and made to justify the first few letters, and Driver suggests that other now long forgotten but once easily remembered words, are supposed to have underlain the order of the remaining. But as he so nicely puts it, 'Even the mnemonic device for the first four letters does some violence to the language'. Driver provides an illustrated graph showing possible linkage of letters in a particular order for a variety of reasons, such as 'Usage, sound of name and usage of sign, meaning of name, sound of name and form of sign, and nature of sound'.

Of course the order might have just developed randomly for no particular reason, or at any rate, no traceable reason, after so many centuries. After all, we have no certain knowledge of how, or precisely where, the letters of the first alphabet originated. John Sassoon (1990), in a paper entitled *Who on Earth invented the Alphabet,* reviewed the relevant literature and presented his own fictional solution.

Whatever the origin, children need to learn the conventional alphabetical order fairly early on in their education in order to look things up in a dictionary or phone book. In educational circles, there is a constant battle between those who believe that the name,

BENGALI

This copybook exercise illustrates some of the simplest combinations that young children must learn. Other more complex combinations are explained in relation to typography in Chapter 9.

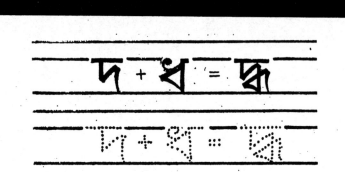

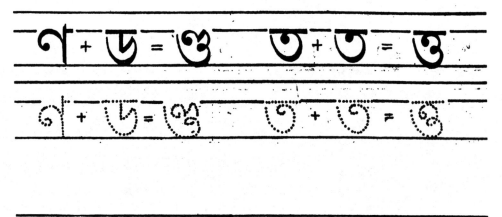

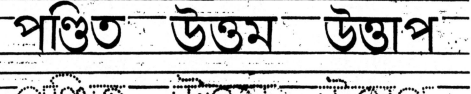

along with the sound of each letter, should be memorised from the start in alphabetical order: 'a' is for (the sound of 'a' in) apple, 'b' is for ball etc., and those who feel that letters for writing, at least, should be taught in stroke related sequences.

This seemingly random alphabetical order contrasts with many other writing systems which often present their letters or characters in a logical or sound–related order. The Japanese syllabaries, Katakana and Hiragana are presented in rectangular grids organised horizontally on the basis of the vowel sounds.

Learning Devanagari
Those who have learned how to write some of the Indian languages, for instance, talk about how 'comforting' it is to chant and memorise the letters and the sounds in their language at the same time in a logical sequence. Trilokesh Mukherjee has written for this chapter a brief description of the development of Devanagari and then shows how this relates to a Bengali child learning to write.

Like most spoken and written languages of India, the Bengali language has developed from a fascinating mixture of Sanscrit language, Devanagari script, the local vernacular dialects and other alpha–numeric variables. By the time Devanagari (or Nagri, as it is often known derived from the word *Nagar* meaning town or city, i.e. the writing system for the city dwellers) letterforms were conceived as visible marks capable of the embodiment of the sounds used in the verbal language. It was possible to carefully plan the structure and matrix of the alphabetic system. An elaborate, sophisticated and systematic grammar, which represented years of debate and discussion, helped. Vernacular languages of India, like Bengali, adapted the same structure, the matrix and many of the grammatical qualities.

Every child who learns to write Bengali appreciates the rudiments of the Bengali letterforms and comes across the baffling unknown new shapes before discovering the connections.

It may not be quite the same to compare the problems of Indian children dealing with ever-increasing complexities as they encounter the different combinations of vowels and consonants with Chinese children learning their characters from the simplest basic strokes to ever more complex ones in a time-honoured sequence. But there are similarities in principle.

Admittedly these are more complex writing systems than the Latin alphabet but over the centuries those who have dealt with them have had a respect for the complexities of their structure and an understanding of the difficulties that learners are likely to encounter.

Models

It may be almost as hard for a writer of the Latin alphabet to adjust to another national model as to learn a new script altogether. Take this rather delightful example of a young English girl who had just learned to write (probably in the separate print script letters that were in general use at the time). Her parents then moved to France for a year. Her early exercises show that she had little problems with the new language or spelling but immense difficulty with the letterforms. It must be said that some of the forms of the model that she was offered were particularly confusing, and her teacher's representation of them did not help. Looking through her books, I could see that she had managed to master this cursive by the end of the year, but it is not difficult to imagine the attitude of her primary school teacher on her return to England. No doubt this child's horizons were widened by her sojourn in France but her handwriting suffered for many years, according to her mother.

It is not possible to prescribe a universal writing model for the Latin alphabet, although so-called experts put forward their own designs of ideal letterforms with disturbing frequency. My own strategy for searching for an optimum model took a different route. My husband, who is very knowledgeable on the subject of handwriting, was involved in a university department which received examination scripts, in English, from all over the world. I asked him to judge which country, in his opinion, submitted the best handwriting. He did not take long to nominate Malaysia. Soon afterwards, on a visit to Kuala Lumpur, I was to meet with the educationists dealing with handwriting policy. Their answer to my query as to what model they employed was a great relief. The reply was that there was no national model. The success of their

Opposite:
This page is taken from the copybook of a young English girl who went to school in France for a year just as she had mastered print script. The top lines are printed in the national model of the time. Underneath is a sample of the teacher's handwriting with the word 'camarade' in particular illustrating his own problems with circular letters. It was not surprising that the poor girl had difficulty following his examples when trying to produce a line of each letter.

A CHILD IN FRANCE

béatrice lit le titre de son livre.

papa va rentrer la voiture.

la   maman   le

papa

camarade

σ σ σ σ δ δ σ σ σ б б б б δ δ φ

a a a a a a a a a a a a a a a a

u u u u u u u u u u u u u

l l l l l l l l l l l l l l l l

d d d d d d d d d d d d d d d d

THE EFFECTS OF MODELS – A HUNGARIAN STUDY

abcdefghijklmno
pqrstuvwxyz
ABCDEFGHIJKLMNO
PQRSTUVWXYZ

*t folyamatos, de egyúttal a szép íráshoz
kéz állandó föl-le mozgás közben eg*

15 éves lány (középiskolás) ▼ „eminens"

*A folyomoto, de egyúttal a nép írásh
hés állondó föl·le morgó köiben egyen*

14 éves fiú (középiskolás) ▼

*A folyamatos, de egyúttal a szé
jobról balra történik m*

15 éves fiú (középiskolás) ▼

Opposite:
Before designing a new model for schools in Hungary, Virágvölgyi (1978) made a study of the effects of several previous models on the handwriting of writers of various ages – in this case a roundhand. This is a constructive way to approach such research.

handwriting policy was the systematic method that was used in all their schools. This took great care over the process of writing, the needs of left-handers and the ductus and heights of letters. If ever there was proof of the old saying that good handwriting is the result of good practice, and that beauty should not be consciously sought – it is here.

Returning to different models of the Latin alphabet: there are considerable differences between writing models within a country, as well as among English speaking countries.There are even more between those who use the Latin alphabet in continental Europe and elsewhere. It is impossible, and maybe undesirable, to reconcile different cultural nuances.

Looking at the whole range of models can be a disconcerting exercise to an uninvolved (but not uncritical) observer. These models can be seen to vary from commercial cursives, based on copperplate, through static print–related models via exaggerated italic hands to truly breathtakingly free aesthetic letters.Whether any one of these can be proven to be more effective than any other in the end remains to be seen.

I despair when I see any group undertake a survey with the intention of altering a model (national, district or even for one school), in the eternal hope that something will magically teach their pupils to write more easily. All too often they alight on some idiosyncratic model that had been introduced with the same fanfare elsewhere some years previously. The researchers depend on the designer's or publisher's idealistic examples as a proof of its success – whereas in all probability by the time it is adopted in country number two, the original country has dropped it as ineffective and gone on to something else.

One of the few studies that illustrates the influence of different national models on the development of mature handwriting is to be found in a modest booklet written by Peter Virágvölgyi (1978). This consists of the research that he undertook before designing a new model for Hungarian schools. It was a good starting point but much more work would need to be done before predicting what is or is not the ideal model in an ever-changing situation.

Models for the writer acquiring a second writing system
How does all this affect students coming to the Latin alphabet as a

second writing system? The model that they are taught may well suit them, but they deserve to know that there are many different styles. Apart from anything else, this will help them to read personal handwriting based on other models. As is evident from the example in Chapter 5, it can be confusing to be made to change to another style and to have to alter your perception as well as your production of written letters. This will be even more so if you have been given the idea that there is only one acceptable way of writing particular letters. Some students may have strong feelings about models and they they may gravitate to one that appears to them to be most aesthetic – or maybe better fitted to their hand and previous training.

Take the example of continuous or commercial cursive – a model still widely used in the US and in continental Europe. To many writers today this is a difficult form of writing. The entry strokes and continuous line date back to a time when pointed (as different from square-cut) quills or pens were used. The entry stroke was needed to initiate the ink-flow and it was not easy to stop and start again mid-word without risking a blob of ink. In order to write this continuous cursive the writer was trained not to rest the whole hand on the desk but only the little finger. The graceful thick and thin strokes of the letters came about from well-trained manipulation of the pressure of the pen – thick, i.e. heavy, downstrokes, then thinup strokes resulting from a release of pressure. Today we need to rest our whole hand on the table in order to control modern writing implements. This makes the writing of copperplate-based cursives awkward at speed, as there is now a need for penlifts to allow the hand to move freely along the page. The entry strokes dictated by the quill are now not necessary. In addition to the unnecessary strain on the hand, the model does not lead to the fast efficient handwriting that students need today.

I had often said, somewhat lightheartedly, that the only students nowadays who could write commercial cursive properly come from China or Japan. At first I put this down to their skill with any writing implement. Then, as illustrated on page 56, another factor soon became evident. Those who learn brush calligraphy are skilled at controlling the writing implement with the hand unsupported. To retain a very light pressure on the paper is

MODELS IN CONTINENTAL EUROPE

Q R S T U V X Y Z

Tomás Ramón León Zamora

Spain

A B C D E F G H

a b c d e f g h

Addentare una mela

Italy

Tu ist nicht im Haus.

Tu ist auch nicht im

Germany

le petit chat joue avec un pétale de tulipe.

papa va rentrer la voiture dans le jardin.

France

MODELS IN CHINA

This is our classroom. It is a big room.

There are two doors and six windows in it.

The walls of the room are white.

On the front wall there is a blackboard.

In South China an italic model was taught in primary schools, as in the example, *left*. In the secondary schools most pupils wrote copperplate. When asked why they had changed, they turned over their old fashioned exercise books. On the back cover there was a copperplate model, *left below*. Students said that they found this more aesthetically pleasing.

印刷正体大小写 Aa Bb Cc Dd Ee

书写斜体大小写 *Aa Bb Cc Dd Ee*

书写圆体大小写 *Aa Bb Cc Dd Ee*

Ff Gg Hh Ii Jj Kk Ll

Ff Gg Hh Ii Jj Kk Ll

Ff Gg Hh Ii Jj Kk Ll

Mm Nn Oo Pp Qq Rr Ss

Mm Nn Oo Pp Qq Rr Ss

Mm Nn Oo Pp Qq Rr Ss

Tt Uu Vv Ww Xx Yy Zz

Tt Uu Vv Ww Xx Yy Zz

Tt Uu Vv Ww Xx Yy Zz

relatively simple for anyone who has undergone such specialised training. Even those who think that they are only concerned with handwriting in their own particular school or district need the wider view that comes from looking at other writing systems.

Different views of the aesthetics of written letters

Things are never simple, as I was to learn in China. Personal tastes can override ergonomics. The young school children in south China were being taught a form of italic handwriting. This was reproduced in their text books and their teachers were excellent proponents as could be seen on the school notice boards. In their class work the nine- and ten-year-old children wrote a clear, consistent but unjoined italic handwriting. Much to my surprise, in the senior school there was no sign of these letterforms. All the pupils were writing continuous commercial cursive. When asked why, they turned over the exercise books, whose cover designs looked as if they had remained unchanged since the 1920s. There was an outdated copperplate alphabet. The students' comment was always the same — 'but these letters are far more beautiful'. Whether considering the writing tool or the model, we must not forget that there are very different ideas of what is aesthetically beautiful in different parts of the world.

北京師范大学第二附属中

I like ball pen best for the aesthetic value it brings to my handwriting. (Chinese characters).

A Chinese student gave this answer to the question: 'Which is the best writing implement?' In other countries the benefits of ballpoint pens and their effects on handwriting are questioned. It seems to be a matter of choice.

Even in Europe there are markedly different ways of viewing the aesthetics of handwriting. Apart from adherence to any national model, some countries put a much higher priority on beautiful handwriting. While this is laudable in one way, there is often a price to pay in terms of the amount of writing a student can produce or the creative content. As a visitor to any country you can never be sure that you are shown representative schools, but in two countries which I have visited recently, the aesthetic standard was very high. In Hungary I watched a class produce beautiful

letterforms in a formal classroom situation. I also noticed from
their books that their written tasks were mostly copying texts or
producing short factual reports. I asked the teacher at what age the
children wrote their own compositions or perhaps poems. The
answer was 'certainly not before the age of ten'. In the school
opposite my home, as in most British primary classrooms, five-
year- olds attempt to write stories and even poems. I cannot say
much for the aesthetic standard of their handwriting, and I doubt if
it would be found acceptable in a Hungarian school. In Sweden I
saw the consequences of such a high aesthetic standard when I
noticed seventeen-year-old students still writing on alternate sets of
staved lines. This meant gives only five or six lines of writing
down the page and very short essays are the result of the
expectation of perfect letterforms.

An English friend resident in Italy told me that his young son
was expected to master four different forms of the alphabet during
his first weeks at school: Printed small letters and plain Roman
capital letters, as well as what he termed 'Script capitals and small
letters based on antiquated vertical copperplate'. These few
examples illustrate how you cannot be sure about the
circumstances that those learning the Latin alphabet will find. It
will depend on which country they are visiting.

What happens in English-speaking classrooms

Occasionally it is possible to pick up useful teaching techniques in
educational books, but not often. They tend to be tediously
conventional. Sometimes imaginative glimpses can be found in
quite unusual places. This delightful excerpt comes from a
biography of Osbert Lancaster (Boston 1989). It describes Mrs
Lancaster's way of teaching her son to read. The author describes
Mrs Lancaster as a tough, capable person, with a sense of humour.
'She was a New Woman, a Shavian and a supporter of votes for
women.' Burton continued: 'Some idea of her originality may be
gathered from the way in which she taught Osbert to read. This
was by means of a chocolate alphabet. Twice a week the edible
letters were spread out on the dining-room table and he was
allowed to eat the letters that he was able to recognise. Once he
had full command of the alphabet he was allowed to eat those
which he could make into a word. By the time he could spell

'suffragette' he was deemed to have mastered literacy by a system of teaching which seemed designed to develop equally a taste for chocolates and long words.' I have used variations of this technique myself to defuse tense situations with problem children. Maybe it gives a new dimension to the phrase 'internalising the letters of the alphabet'.

On a more serious level, there is usually something to be learned by watching any experienced teacher at work in a classroom, particularly one who has developed his or her own techniques or teaching aids. In cross-cultural matters, concerned with handwriting at least, these opportunities are not so common. Not long ago I was in a teachers' centre looking at the details of a term-long course on multi-lingualism in the classroom. I saw no mention of dealing with a second writing system, despite the large population of children in the district who would have to learn another writing system as well as a second language. The tutor became quite defensive when questioned about whether this subject was tackled, and retorted that I should talk to the director if I had any complaints. This was hardly the response that I had expected.

This way of indicating the height differentials was found in a German child's exercise book.

In a short article, Dunn (1984) states: 'Once children who already write in their own language begin to learn English, they are generally eager to get on and write in English. To be able to write in English provides written proof of progress for both children and their parents. This gives satisfaction that motivates.' I would not argue with that, but find the rest of the article not to be of much use in the aspects which I consider to be important. The only paragraph that hints at any possible problems (and then dismisses them) is as follows: 'Teachers are often worried that children who already write in a different script from *bottom to top of the page* (Japanese/Chinese) or right to left across the page (Arabic) will have difficulty in writing in Roman script. [The italics are my own, I feel that this is just a printing error – but an unfortunate one.] From what I have observed, children learn amazingly quickly, taking the change – to left to right across the page – quite naturally. It is generally adults who find it difficult, as they are more fixed in their movements and attitudes. It is important for teachers to be careful not to transmit any feeling of difficulty or apprehension.'

It is with this last statement that I would argue. It might be acceptable if the teachers were to be truly informed of all the possible difficulties, and on the lookout for those that might be expected. If not, this would not be a helpful attitude to take. Directionality by itself is one matter, the hand positions involved in the scripts with different movements is another – just as important. See page 60 for the examples of Arabic teachers' handwriting and experiences. A short time ago I had the opportunity to give a talk to nearly a hundred bilingual (Hebrew-English) school leavers. In front of their head teacher, the 17 to 19-year-olds almost all raised their hands when asked if the act of writing was painful for them When I phrased it another way, precisely four of them put up their hands to indicate that writing either in English or Hebrew was comfortable and pain-free.

Shortly after I also gave a talk to the 50 or so teachers of their school. I tackled the somewhat disbelieving teaching staff on this issue of pain, and was challenged vociferously when I asked whether they showed their pupils the different hand positions needed for the different directions of handwriting. When the clamour died down, just one experienced teacher supported me saying: 'I have taught writing for 20 years and always demonstrate the two hand positions.' So I set the teachers the same task as I had set the Arabic teachers and was interested to hear afterwards from one teacher (only) that of course she altered hand positions between alphabets but had never realised it before. This is just what I wanted to hear. Nothing about the act of writing is natural: it is a taught skill and teachers need to be aware of how to deal with the important issues that arise between writing systems – and not just to discount them as obvious.

What can be learned from techniques in other countries
There is a great deal to learn from the way other cultures teach both their own writing system and the Latin alphabet. The illustrations on page 56 and in this chapter are just a few examples that I can reproduce in this book. Occasionally you can find some good ideas in unexpected places. I was in the Solomon Islands recently and was lent a modest book called *Aloha Solomons* by Gwen Cross. It was so battered that any evidence of date or publisher had been obliterated but there were some wise

These illustrations remind young children of the basic shapes of Chinese characters.

comments about how she had taught writing to the islanders. 'I encouraged them to make the letters (consonants) to hang separately on thin wood, so that they could introduce new letters in the order and language they needed. Later they would add pictures illustrating the vowel sounds. Empty packing cases were in great demand.'

Of her Melanesian pupils she had some astute observations to make: 'They had very exact sight and great concentration – looking, remembering and imitating. Melanesians learn from early childhood how to observe very carefully since in the bush, and on the shore, on the reef and in the sea good and bad things abound around them.' Gwen Cross had invented a consonantal alphabet and a way of teaching that worked well because most consonants are international while vowels, when pronounced, vary with the language.

Having met some delightful island children, and visited their schools, there is more to say. Their discipline, their respect of education and all involved in it is still obvious. We visited a school which consisted of a group of open-sided, palm-thatched huts in a jungle clearing. With a minimum of books and no visible equipment, this school was producing articulate children with a sense of adventure and intellectual curiosity that was impressive.

Appropriateness of content

There was another lesson to be learned from Cross's book, which is not directly concerned with handwriting but too valuable to omit. 'We cannot speak English which conveys the message we intend unless the words we use contain an understanding of the cultural pattern of the listeners. For one is not even aware of one's European culture until one has truly experienced a culture that is not European.' This paragraph appeared after an anecdote describing how a visiting speaker used unfamiliar words and concepts that even the interpreter could not understand or reproduce.

Similar thoughts were expressed by Cooper (1994) in a modest journal entitled *Notes on Literacy*. In an article entitled Look Before the Pencil Leaps, Cooper, a linguistic consultant working in Papua New Guinea, points out: 'By not having made an in-depth comparison of the relationship between oral and written discourse styles, the outside "expert" can be lulled into a faulty analysis of the relationship, both by his own and by mother-tongue speaker perceptions.... When we teach writing skills before we learn where the students are coming from, we may distort the features of their cultural and linguistic grid and in the process make the results less meaningful, and perhaps totally irrelevant or inaccessible to the audience we believe we are serving.'

I have fought several battles over the appropriateness of multi-cultural pupil material and have not always won. Why, for example, should handwriting exercises for children from very different cultures consist of copying out totally inappropriate European nursery rhymes, as is often the case?

This concept of appropriateness can be extended further. Eade (1994) explains his theory of 'indigenous visual convention'. His own writings extend this theory of graphic conventions much more widely than is possible in this book – to the use of colour, for instance. What he has to say about the lack of graphic quality in literacy primers (here in relation to African minority languages) is equally relevant to materials for teaching handwriting. His findings include: 'My first conclusion is that indigenous visual conventions exist, and that they vary from one ethnic group to another. They warrant careful examination by literacy workers, in particular, and educationists in general. My second conclusion is that from the point of view of the pre-literate, learning to read can often be hindered by the illegibility of the materials used.' To Eade's words I would like to add the idea of appropriateness of illustrative material. Very few designers seriously consider the likely tastes of children from their own culture, much less from another.

Materials
Back to the more practical issues. There is a great deal to be learned from the materials used in other countries. I have seen spiral pencils and square ones as well as the more usual triangular ones, all of which come from Japan. The spiral ones in particular give children an ideal surface to hold.

Educational suppliers stock different types of triangular pen grips that purport to correct penhold (these are quite common in Great Britain and the United States) – assuming that all penholds should be similar for all writing implements. In China I was presented with a pack of far more ingenious plastic pen grips. Not content with those that keep the fingers in the prescribed position on a pencil, the Chinese had slightly different ones for ballpoint pen, crayon and brush. The user is able to feel the subtle differences required to get the best out of different writing implements. In inexpensive Chinese copybooks it is possible to see how teachers are shown how to write on the blackboard, and the detail in which different pencil and penholds are described is remarkable.

In Hong Kong the cheapest copybooks, if that was what they could be called, worked in a practical way that recognised the need for many children to practise of any set of characters more than once. There were folded sheets of cheap tracing paper made up into booklets, sold with model strips that fitted inside the double pages. As well as being economical, this technique solved one of the problems that I associate with tracing. The master sheet would be held so securely that the clumsiest youngster would find it easy to work with.

In Malaysia I saw practical and inexpensive cardboard cut-outs for teaching the basic strokes of Chinese characters. I would like to see someone produce something similar for other languages.

I have seen many different ways of helping children to judge the quality of their own writing, and of course, there is much more to learn from how other writing systems are taught. By observing them you might end up with a better understanding of how to teach your own script – and maybe language, spelling and grammar, as well.

PERSONAL LETTERS IN PRINT

Terengganu, Malaysia.

The way that people see an alphabet can often be studied via printed rather than informally written forms. This can give new insight into how letters of the Latin alphabet can be manipulated but still retain their identity. The top example is from the east coast of Malaysia. The Arabic influence is evident. The broken descenders, resembling Chinese brush strokes, in the central example, as well as the italic flourishes below, suggest that they were the work of Chinese calligraphers.

CHAPTER 7

Handwriting and Personality

If your handwriting is partly what you have been taught and partly what you are, then learning a second writing system might add another dimension of variability to personal letterforms.

At a certain stage in learning a new writing system some characters are likely to resemble those in the writer's first one. How long this lasts is worthy of further study and would be of interest to forensic examiners. Some such personal variations might puzzle those involved in computer recognition of writing because it is relatively simple to decipher personal variations from a familiar model, but those from an unfamiliar one may cause problems – those related to other writing systems are uncharted territory.

How long such variations related to a first writing system might persist could depend on a variety of factors. The first would be that the maybe writers might not even notice them. Some characteristic variations could be the result of the writer's ingrained motor movements as illustrated on p. 46, in which case these might well become permanent, but other more subtle forces might also be at work. Consciously or unconsciously there might be a desire to retain the flavour of the writer's own culture and with it those special differences. The Latin alphabet is flexible, and there is no reason to assume automatically that such variations would disrupt the reader. Where legibility is not affected perhaps we should welcome the addition of such variations – and certainly not set out to destroy such manifestations in beginners' work.

Graphology

The subject of personality and handwriting has been studied for centuries. Jacoby (1939) reports, in a survey of graphological writing, that the first detailed work on the relation between handwriting and personality was published in 1622 – *Trattato come da una lettera missiva si cognosca la natura e la qualita della scritore.* Western graphological studies started seriously in France, when as Jacoby, one of the most influential graphologists in this century tells us, 'The most significant step in the advance of graphology was taken in France during the second half of the last century, by the Abbe Michon who in 1871 introduced the word graphology ... and between the 1895 and 1920 methodical investigation of the psychology of handwriting resulted in the establishment of graphology as a science.' Jacoby, in a somewhat Eurocentric way, starts his first chapter with these sentences, 'The science of graphology is commonly believed to be an entirely modern one. Actually it has a history of almost seventy years and the notion of a connection between handwriting and personality can be traced to antiquity'. He later redeems himself somewhat by suggesting, 'Even in graphological circles it is little known that many centuries ago, in the East, especially the Chinese, possessed insight into the psychology of handwriting.'

The Chinese tradition of graphology
It was with great interest, therefore, that I listened to a presentation in Brussels by Menasse-Cremers who, with Chinese colleagues, has founded the International Institute for Scientific Research in Chinese Graphology. The Institute's main aim is to undertake 'historical research into Chinese graphology for the purpose of identifying the contribution made by the cultural heritage of China in a field where Chinese thought has proved particularly productive'. In a joint presentation with Xu Jianping, the long history of graphological thought in China was brought into perspective. Yang Xiong (53 BC–18 AD) was quoted as saying that; 'The words that we utter are the voice of our spirit, the characters we

Opposite:
It is usual for those beginning to learn a second writing system to retain the flavour of their first. This is illustrated by the square forms of a Tamil pupil while below are some examples from Punjabi children in London schools.

write are its paintings. This voice and this painting reveal the interiority of human nature.' Words written during the first century AD by Zhang Huai-guan were translated to reveal his views which are as relevant today as they were then: 'One must read several lines of a text before one can understand the thinking of its author. With handwriting, one requires but a single character to know the mind of the writer.' I am grateful to Mme Menasse-Cremers for permitting me to quote so widely from her fascinating paper because I could not resist the table that she has translated by the calligrapher Xiang Mu from the Ming Dynasty. The table relates twelve characteristics of the personality of the writer and opposite them lists characteristics of their handwriting. If I quote just a few of my favourites from that list, you will be able to judge how astute his descriptions were:

Crafty Hypocritical	too chiselled, too careful
Amiable or a manipulator	irregular
Frank and unswerving	firm and prompt
Prudent, stable, poised	lack of originality

I am not a graphologist and have explained why in *The Art and Science of Handwriting* (1993) I would side with my late friend Ruth Mock, who wrote with Gordon in 1960: 'Long after death, as vividly as the day on which it was written, handwriting tells of the person's individuality, thoughts and impulses, for the physical manipulation of the pen and the graphic shapes which we make are determined by all the qualities and experiences which form our personalities.' Ruth Mock understood handwriting as few others did in the 1960s but she was not a graphologist. She was an art teacher and her co-author a school inspector.

Personal variations and attitudes

I cannot help but be interested, not only in personal variations in handwriting or calligraphy, but in attitudes towards them. When introduced to Chinese calligraphy at first hand by an elderly scribe in Malaysia (just before visiting mainland China) I was given a demonstration of the 18 classical hands that are the essential basic repertoire of a calligrapher even today. But, from the very beginning, as I listened to connoisseurs discussing national treasures, in Xian and elsewhere, I became aware of the value placed on personal variations or interpretations of these classical styles. Of this Xiang writes: 'Calligraphy is like a face – it differs from one person to another depending on the spirit the individual projects from inside to the outside. That is why calligraphers all possess their own personal style, even if they practise the same style of calligraphy.' For Xiang, I suspect, calligraphy and handwriting were synonymous. How I wish that Western calligraphers would appreciate his point instead of arrogantly imposing on their unfortunate students their own (often imperfect) personal interpretations of classic styles. There is, of course, a basic difference between the writing systems of the two cultures. Latin calligraphy consists of copying styles that were once everyday handwriting, while popular handwriting styles are still developing and constantly altering. The more fortunate Chinese are still writing, although with modern implements, the same characters that have stood the test of many centuries.

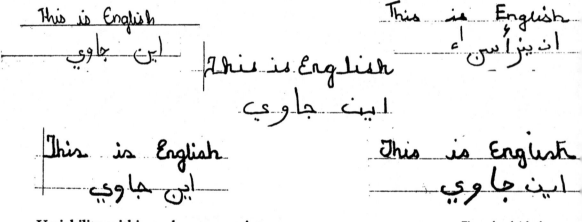

Variability within and among scripts

Variability among writers surely exists to a certain extent in all writing systems. In the past, traditional teaching methods may have kept this somewhat in check. Now that handwriting has been supplanted as the universal means of business communication, at least, by the keyboard, a more relaxed attitude to teaching models has started to spread. With the increase of personal freedom, and the emphasis shifting to more creativity in schools and in society in general, interesting trends can be traced worldwide. From readers'

Five schoolgirls show how the personal characteristics of their written trace are constant between their English and Arabic handwriting.

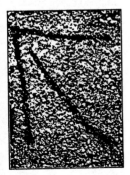

This informally written combination of 'aert' in Flemish would probably confuse English speakers, who would read this as the more familiar 'ant'.

Muylaert-Hofman

Capital letters also show national as well as personal variations. Notice particularly the 'K's from Indonesia, one formal and one taken from graffiti.

point of view this means that there are not going to be uniform characters in any particular group of writers. When they are not yet familiar with a language and alphabet here, there may be some difficulty in deciphering personal scripts.

Personal handwriting can also be difficult to decipher when written in the same alphabet, but a different language. This is often caused by the way people automate and simplify the common letter strings that occur in their own language. The word 'the' in English often becomes a personal hieroglyph, losing the form of individual letters, or, for example, the word-endings like 'ing' or 'ant'. Consider another language, in this case Flemish, with the common letter combination of 'aert'. You can imagine from this advertisement (see left) that any English speakers, unfamiliar with the Flemish language, would probably read that name as Muylant (that is if they had deciphered the unfamiliar first part of the name correctly) rather than Muylaert.

It is not difficult to show how certain personal characteristics transcend different alphabets or systems. This strengthens the traditional graphological theories and certainly ties up with my own less complex ones: that your handwriting is a reflection of yourself on paper, and a result of the way you use the hand that wields the pen – and your whole body. Unless distorted by additional tensions involved in using another language, it is hardly surprising that personal characteristics, and a certain flavour, are retained within the production of a second writing system. I would just like to present a few examples to illustrate this point.

My Dearest

Hello! Ho
I'm sorry I ha
And Thank yo
  Now I'm a
has already t
another girl.
nese girl.)

    So I'm g
next heartbn
    It is ve

Anyway

— I have a lo
  to tell you.

May the goo.

Next Year is A Year of Rabbit. in Japan.

Writing and illustration from a twenty-year-old Japanese boy and *opposite:* two Japanese children's illustrations.

Handwriting and teenagers

A feature that has been noticed for several decades in Great Britain is the emergence of teenage peer-group scripts. Ruth Mock remarked in 1960: 'Secondary school children especially are given to forms of self-assertion – it is part of the process of growing up, of measuring themselves against society, and of trying to find their place in it. They become self-conscious about their speech, dress and behaviour, and idiosyncrasies belonging to someone else whom they admire, often appear in their handwriting. These are in due course either rejected or assimilated into their own style, but for a time they are obtrusive, as are ornate signatures and other characteristics consciously assumed.'

Some thirty years later, the cult of the teenager has become more pronounced. My own observations have gone further, not only from looking at the written trace as reported in Sassoon (1993), but looking in particular at the rounded and idiosyncratic forms that seem to have resulted from alterations in perception and writing implements. In addition, in my opinion, these forms are the result of more aggressive use of the body. I was fascinated to hear a presentation by an old friend, Professor Yoshiaki Nihei, at the 25th International Congress of Psychology in Brussels. It was on precisely the same subject – *Handwriting as a Social Act: The Rise and Fall of Anti-Calligraphic Handwriting in Japan.*

Nihei proposed that handwriting could be regarded as a social act and that the selection of a style can be a confirmation of social identity. He continued: 'In Japan unique forms of handwriting have developed by different social groups to assert their particular character. The type of bold writing called Geba-ji used often by

radical student groups, is one example while the stylised writings used in the Kabuki billboard is another.'

Nihei continued with the main thrust of his argument which is most relevant here: 'However in the last 15 years or so, among Japanese female teenagers, an especially interesting type of handwriting has emerged that demonstrates a drastic deviation from the recommended style of handwriting at school. This writing commonly called "manga–ji" (comic like letters) or "maru–moji" (roundish letters), has come to represent the unique characteristics of the culture of teenage girls.' He goes on to explain how, 'Schoolchildren, after formal calligraphic education from the third grade, are usually recommended to write in a calligraphy-based style that retains elements of the calligraphic movement (CBS). The anti-calligraphic style (ACS) has met with criticism from journalists as well as educationists and has become a social problem as girls continue to use this style despite being prohibited to do so by their teachers.'

This comment reminds me of an incident in a local secondary school near where I live in England. The head teacher told me that she had become infuriated by her teenage girls' habit of putting a large circle over the letter 'i' instead of a neat dot. She said that she was considering banning this practice. For what it was worth, I advised her against it, saying as I remember, that it was about as much good as banning measles. No ban would succeed as the habit was in itself a sign of immaturity and would disappear in time.

Nihei's study had looked at matters in detail and he reported that during the 80s the style became a 'submerged culture' in

CALLIGRAPHIC AND ANTI-CALLIGRAPHIC STYLES

あいうえおか
きくけこさし
すせそたちつ
てとなにぬね
のはひふへほ
まみむめもや
ゆよらりるれ
ろわをんじで

あいうえおか
きくけこさし
すせそたちつ
てとなにぬね
のはひふへほ
まみむめもや
ゆよらりるれ
ろわをんじで

Above: the characters written with a calligraphic word processor (Fuji Software Co.).
Top right: the characters written in 'calligraphy-based style'.
Right: the characters written in 'anti-calligraphic style'.

Illustrations from Nihei (1992). Handwriting as a social act: the rise and fall of an anti-calligraphic style of handwriting in Japan.

あいうえみな
きくけこさし
すせせたちつ
ことなにぬね
のほひふへほ
まみむめもや
ゆよらりるも
ろちをんじを

that the young writers distinguished their private experience from their public experience, using a different handwriting according to their situations. They used the anti-calligraphic style in such private situations as personal letters and diaries. In such formal situations as examinations and notebooks to be submitted to teachers, they used the calligraphy-based style which their teachers recommended.

I find these reports most interesting and somewhat in contrast to what is happening in Great Britain, where I have made many observations, and in the United States and Australia, where similar aspects of teenage fashions can be observed in varying degrees. Here we recommend to girls to keep their teenage peer-group style for personal use only, but to no avail. As there is perhaps less parental control in Western countries than in Japan, and less teacher influence over such matters, young people do not seem to alter their handwriting between personal and public writing. It is almost as if they cannot, it has become so much of their persona. The only means that I have found of showing such students how to break out of their teenage style is to make them write at high speed – almost a scribble. Then their writing is often much more mature, flowing and compressed as well as forward slanting. This maturity seemed to happen unconsciously as far as can be ascertained, and also can be seen to appear in their signatures. My conclusions are that the maturity and efficiency are being inhibited by social, peer-group and educational influences and expectations. This is reported in my book *The Art and Science of Handwriting*.

Nihei analyses the characteristics of the anti-calligraphic style:

1 Both the contours of letters and strokes are transformed uniformly into roundish ones.
2 Parts of each character are simplified, loosing the trace of the CBS.
3 Curves are exaggerated.
4 Angles are undermined.
5 Each letter is written in a discrete hand, differing from the CBS in which letters are occasionally presented in the continuum
6 Girls who use the ACS uniformly describe the impression of ACS as "cute".

This concept of 'cuteness' is one that interests me. I am by no means the first to recognise such signs in Japanese children in their drawings. I have also seen the same manifestations in their handwriting in English. The writing with its accompanying illustration here is from a Japanese boy, not a girl, and he was aged about twenty years old. Younger children at the same time (the late 1980s) seemed to be illustrating their written work in a similarly 'cute' style.

Anyone interested in the detailed data will have to apply to Professor Nihei himself, but his analysis of the factors contributing to the use of the ACS cannot be left out of this abstract of his fascinating paper:

Factors in motor control
    Simplification of motor control
    Matching with the direction of writing
    Characteristic of writing instrument (increased use of mechanical pencils)
Factors in learning
    Facility in learning
Socio-cultural factors
    Cuteness as a paradigm,
    Rejection of maturation by girls
Personality factors
    Social extroversion (need of joining a peer group)
    Rhathmya (seeking new stimulation).

A noticeable alteration from taught letterforms has always been the sign of strong personalities. A deviation noticeable across a wide proportion of a generation in any country, or set of countries, is an interesting study which can give us pointers to changing attitudes to educational and cultural stances between generations. In writing systems in transition it is sometimes possible to discern other indications of generation differences. The Japanese – and the Chinese to a lesser extent – have long been setting type from left to right, and sometimes writing in either direction along the line instead of in columns downward from right to left. It interested me therefore to be told by a young man in Hong Kong that if he were writing to his grandfather he would still write in the traditional way in downward columns, as a mark

Some professions seem to have adopted styles of their own. This illustration was produced by Don Hatcher, an Australian graphic designer.

of respect. For his own friends he would write from right to left along the line. We are not thinking in this instance, of the directional confusion that such a transitional period might produce in China or Japan, but of directionality as an indicator of mood or modernity, or even of manners.

The Art Directors hand is something like this with characters much rounder than the calligrapher's hand. Staff who write in a very similar style to this with some using the 2 rather than a.
This style is quite different to the drafting hand with its upright emphasis and exaggerated ascenders and descenders for example... Because of the accepted style everyone ends up writing in a similar style to this. Very wide letters, very little space between letters and very tall ascending strokes.

One wrote like this — rather wild dots and one with gigantic x height and exaggerated roundness.

Nyohitsu, *c.*1730, hiragana, 'women's calligraphy',
reproduced from Gaur (1994).

CHAPTER 8

Handwriting, Society and Politics

Different cultures view the act of writing in different ways. In some countries, letters are just the means of delivering the message, while in others there are spiritual overtones or aesthetic values to be considered. In some societies it is conformity that is valued; in others, individuality. In addition, the level of writing or even the model can also have political implications.

With some scripts, notably Chinese and Arabic, it is difficult to separate the concept of calligraphy from everyday handwriting, so deep are the effects of the traditional respect for the act of writing.The religious implications of Arabic writing is explained by Safadi (1978) in his book on Arabic calligraphy. 'It must be emphasised that the Qur'an has always played a central role in the development of Arabic script. The need to record the Qur'an precisely compelled the Arabs to reform their script and to beautify it so that it became worthy of the divine revelation.'

Buland al-Hadieri (1981) explains how other styles and modes of innovative execution of the Kufic script spread and how the richness and widespread extent of its many forms and styles can be ascribed to the religious emotion with which Muslims regard the written word. He explains further: 'The spread of Islam to the East and West, and the acceptance of it by many peoples, and the attempts by each region to distinguish it by its own particular script, has had an important effect on the number of types it has and the wealth of its styles.' Although it may not be particularly relevant to this chapter I very much like his description of the Arabic script which might be appropriate for many others as well : 'It moves, yet it moves not.'

Lubell (1990) ties Hebrew to its biblical origins. He explains how the medieval mystical scholar, Moses de Leon, wrote on the origins of the Hebrew alphabet: 'Twenty-six generations before the creation of the world, the twenty-two letters of the alphabet descended from the crown of God whereon they were engraved with a pen of flaming fire.' Lubell cites Wilson (1978) for a modern view of Hebrew as seen by a non-Hebrew speaker. Again the tie between religion and the alphabet is stressed: 'These twenty-two signs that Moses was believed to have brought back from Egypt graven on the Tables of the Law... in the Bible take on an aspect exalted and somewhat mysterious. The square letters holding their course, with no capitals for proper names, and no punctuation save for the firm double diamond that marks the end of the verse... while above and below them a dance of accents shows the pattern of the metrical structure and rise and fall of the chanting.'

David (1990) provides a short essay on the history of Hebrew writing in a book primarily aimed at calligraphers, conveying the richness of styles in which Hebrew has been rendered throughout the centuries. What he says about the relationship of Hebrew writing with the Jewish heritage fits well into this chapter. David contrasts Hebrew to the Latin alphabet, which he describes as becoming less formal during the last centuries of the first millennium. He explains: 'In Hebrew the trend is reversed. Because the Jewish people had lost their national independence and many of their cultural institutions, they were left with only their spiritual inheritance. This inheritance had to be guarded, preserved and protected. Hebrew letters, therefore, did not become less formal; instead they became more refined.'

In countries using the Latin alphabet neither aesthetic nor spiritual attitudes to the act of writing have been an important part of the culture. The Latin alphabet spread across Europe as Christianity itself spread. However the written trace was not held in particular respect. It was – and maybe still is – considered only as a means of conveying a message. Until very recently, in any reference to the beauty of handwritten books of hours and other products of the scriptoria from the monastic era, the praise was reserved for the drawn and painted illuminations that decorated such manuscripts, not the letters themselves.

Specialist scripts
From time to time, special groups within many societies have developed exclusive scripts for a variety of purposes. Take women, for instance: Gaur (1994), in her book *The History of Calligraphy* explains how, at the time of the Heian Dynasty (794-1192) in

Kanteiryu (Kantei-style) is used in posters of Japanese traditional entertainments and a traditional sport, from Nihei (1992).

Japan, the lives of a small group of courtiers revolved almost exclusively around aesthetic and creative activities, above all, calligraphy. She details the styles used: 'While the serious matters of state and religion were conducted by men who continued to write in Kanji, or *Onokode* (men's writing), women composed their novels, poems and the all-important love letters in an elegant and graceful hiragana which was known as *Onnade* (women's writing).' The example of women's calligraphy c. 1730 is reproduced from Gaur (1994).

Another possible example was reported recently in The China Daily (1986). Professor Gong Zhibing, a linguistic scholar, had, according to an article reprinted in the Daily Yomiuru (June 2 1986), discovered an ancient writing system 'for women only' believed to date back more than 2000 years. The script used an inverted system of grammar and syntax and resembles Shang dynasty (1600-1100 BC) oracle bone carvings and Quin dynasty (221-206 BC) characters. Local sources reported that this writing, which mothers taught their daughters at home, had been invented by a lonely concubine in the Song dynasty (960-1270). They believe that she brought it back to her home town in Hunan, where it is still in use.

Gong found two women in their eighties who were still able to read and write the script. He believes that the system was too complicated to have been invented by one woman alone. His explanation is that women had preserved for their own use relics of a writing system thought to have vanished when Quinshi Huangdi, the first emperor, united China in 221 BC. He laid the foundations of a united Chinese script by forbidding the use of all writing except in his official 'small seal' characters.

Language and writing
Many alphabets, Latin for example, are unlikely to suit all subsequent languages. Alphabets on the whole did not follow languages but were the result of political decisions. However, once adopted, a writing system cannot always be separated from language. Perhaps the best known example of this is the use of Chinese characters by the Japanese. This was largely completed between the fifth and ninth centuries, and by now is so deeply entrenched that it has become an essential tradition within Japanese

culture. Gaur (1994) explains: 'Since there exist, however, hardly
any similarities between the agglutinative, polysyllabic Japanese and
the largely monosyllabic Chinese language, the adoption of the
Chinese script did present serious problems.' Various solutions
were developed such as special notations which were required to
indicate the order in which individual characters had to be
read.Two syllabaries were added. These were derived from
calligraphic forms of Chinese characters and were developed and
simplifyied over several centuries. Hiragana is widely used today
and many words can be written entirely by it. Katakana is less in
use, and is confined for the most part to transcription of foreign
words. As Gaur explains: 'So Japanese can be written in more than
one way, in Chinese characters, (*Kanji*), in syllabic characters
specially designed to represent the Japanese language, and in a
combination of both. This multiplicity of forms allowed for the
creation of unique elements in Japanese calligraphy.'

One Japanese-speaking scholar tried to explain to me how he
views this relationship of the language as represented by Kanji:
'Think of a concept without a word and no sound.' These writers
are both Europeans explaining Japanese for a European audience.
A Japanese writer might not use the same words at all.

The place of the writer in society

This is perhaps a good place to discuss the different attitudes and
functions of those who undertake the act of writing in different
cultures – to separate the calligrapher from the scribe, and the
scribe from the individual writer. Traditionally the calligrapher,
particularly in Chinese culture, was held in great respect. His skill
added extra depth and meaning to the written word, elevating it
above the mere passing of a message.

In early civilisations scribes controlled the machinery of
government, education and literature. Ancient societies could be
described as scribe-led or managed and scribes wielded immense
power. By the Middle Ages, in Europe at least, the scribe had been
relegated to the position of a copyist. A mediaeval scribe in his
scriptorium was not greatly lauded at the time. It is only in
retrospect that his work is analysed and praised as an art form. The
scribe, as different from the illuminator, held a much lower
position in society than an Arabic or Chinese calligrapher. As

someone performing a useful function in illiterate or semi-literate societies, he would be elevated above the general populace but that is all. In the social hierarchy the scribe became a clerk, a tradesman and certainly not an aristocrat, not even a gentleman.

It was only after the advent of printing, which freed the scribe and copyist from the tedium of producing books and allowed the spread of learning, that to be able to write 'a fair hand' became the mark of a gentleman in European culture. Over the years this altered. So-called gentlemen in Victorian England steered clear of a perfect hand lest they be confused with a mere clerk whose livelihood depended on just that perfect script. One of my favourite quotations (from Thoyts 1893) is this: 'To sum up the matter briefly, it will be observed that a clever person cares very little about the form of his writing – it is the matter alone which concerns him; whereas with a limited brainpower great care as to appearance is taken.' Thoyts was writing of another age, but I think that this is a fair assumption of the attitude of many Western academics today. This attitude could not be further away from the attitude of a Chinese scholar and is a way of thinking which might also cause misunderstanding between those in other cultures.

Handwriting and society

It is undeniable that literacy is a political issue – to write is to be empowered. To be semi-literate is not enough and above all to be able only to read enables you only to take in what others wish you to read. To be able to write enables people to express their ideas and present their views to the world.

The way that countries deal with immigrant populations differ considerably. Policies may reflect a nation's attitude, at any particular time, to those wishing to settle in their country. In those countries which traditionally attracted immigrants – America in particular and also Australia to a certain extent – a strong national handwriting model was encouraged during the last century. In this way a visible part of a new national identity was forged. Although Australia has now broken away from the copperplate-based letterforms of the last century, the USA has still to make a concerted effort to do so.

Where assimilation takes place forcibly after conquest, other methods have proved successful throughout history. Many

GERMAN HANDWRITING: GOTHIC AND ROMAN

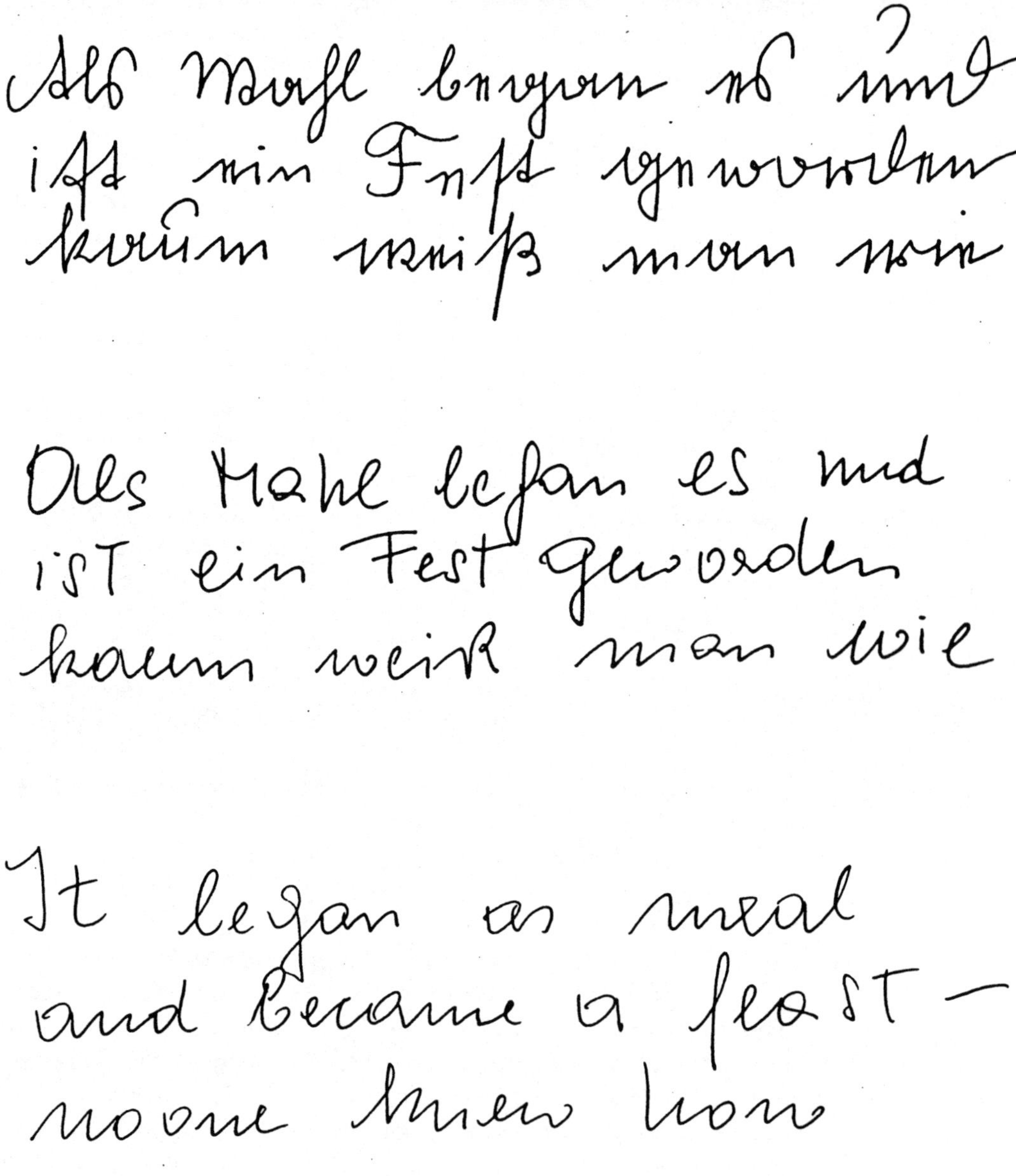
Als Mahl begann es und
ist ein Fest geworden
kaum weiß man wie
Als Mahl begann es und
ist ein Fest geworden
kaum weiß man wie
It began as meal
and became a feast —
noone knew how

Opposite:
A quotation from *Der Kornett* by Rainer Maria Rilke, written out by Dr Albertine Gaur. First it is written in German in Gothic letters then in German in the Latin alphabet and then translated into English.

civilisations, from ancient times, had varying levels of their written scripts, from an everyday hand for general purposes via a more formal script for government usage up to the level reserved for religious purposes. By repressing the highest level of writing it was, and still is, possible to ensure that within a few generations a people will no longer have access to a large part of their own separate written heritage. As Fred Eade said to me: 'A legitimate script facilitates a legitimate speaker or text. Suppression of the script, therefore, means peripheralising speakers of the language(s) that use that script.' He gave the examples of Kurdish in Iran, Iraq and Turkey; Tibetan; Arabic in transcriptions into the Latin alphabet in West Africa; and finally Gaelic.

In countries which accept a large proportion of immigrants today there is a difficult balance to retain. This balance is between emphasing the importance of retaining the writing system of their culture and religion while not retarding the learning and usage of the new language and writing system.

In many cases this balance is also a personal decision and goes deeper than just speaking and writing. An Indian colleague who came to Britain during her childhood explained it to me this way: Although she had lived in England for most of her life, when occasionally she had reason to use the writing system of her childhood she reverted also to that persona.

Handwriting and politics

The issue of handwriting and politics deserves a wider perspective. Dr Albertine Gaur has contributed the next section. Her expertise in the field of handwriting studies is reflected in her wide range of books on the subject. Her work has been of great use to me in the preparation of this book (Gaur 1979, 1986, 1994), and her advice at various stages of the writing has been invaluable.

'Writing systems are essential elements of the political infrastructure. They either emerge within a particular society when the need arises, if there is no indigenous system in place an alien one might be adopted, or a system might simply be imposed in the course of (religious or political) colonisation. After the fall of Rome in the 5th century AD the Roman alphabet followed Christianity into Europe. A millennium later it spread, together with printing, to all parts of the world where Western civilisation extended its

FRAGMENTS SAVED FROM A TIBETAN BONFIRE

A Tibetan boy walks to school with with his slate
slung over his shoulder.

TIBET – HANDWRITING FROM VARIOUS SOURCES

U-Chen (dBu. cän)
Tibetan formal script
Written by right-hander
with left-hand italic nib

TIBETAN HANDWRITING

ཟྃ tuurmank

Ka	KHA	GA	NGA	CHA	CHÄ	JA	NA
TA	THA	DHA	NA	PA	PHA	BHA	MA
CHA	CHÄ	JA	WH	SH	JA	HA	YA
RA	ð LA	SHA	SA			HA	AÄ

influence. Arabic, as the sacred script of the Qur'an, became, after the 7th century, the spiritual and administrative backbone of the farflung Islamic states. The Chinese script has, since the early part of the Christian millennium, dominated communications in the Far East and successfully served as a medium of information storage even for languages for which it was totally unsuited (e.g. Japanese). In all cases there were advantages and disadvantages. On the one end of the spectrum, new systems could stimulate literacy and encourage development, but on the other end not only existing writing systems but whole languages were lost.

'Attempts at deciphering Maya writing have been made since the 16th century when the script was first discovered. Yet today, after several, often highly imaginative attempts, we can with certainty hardly read more than calendar signs and notational symbols. The main reason lies in the religious fervour of the Spanish Conquistadores and their accompanying Jesuit priests, who not only destroyed inscriptions and documents (in fact only three Maya manuscripts have survived), but also omitted from their dictionaries all terms referring to Maya religion and Maya ritual. In consequence, despite the fact that the language is still spoken in parts of Central America, the key to Maya culture and Maya history has eluded us.

'In Vietnam the Chinese script was first introduced in the 2nd century AD and stayed until the beginning of the 20th century. In the 17th century, however, Jesuit missionaries, who had already worked (though with little lasting success), on the romanisation of Chinese and Japanese, devised a romanised scheme for the publication of Christian texts, dictionaries and eventually also grammars. French colonial rule led to a diffusion of this script (ironically called 'national language' – *quoc ngu*) throughout the country. In 1865 the first Vietnamese newspaper was printed in quoc ngu and in 1910 the script was made compulsory. A generous number of diacritics (often more than one for a single letter) and modified letters are necessary to represent the sounds, tones and accents of the Vietnamese language. But though this foreign-devised Vietnamese alphabet has often been called a printer's nightmare, and is not even particularly legible, it is easier to learn than the innumerable and complicated Chinese characters and has, in consequence, increased literacy.

'In Turkey the change of writing system was not imposed from
the outside, but it was nevertheless a highly political decision. In
1928 Mustafa Kemal Ataturk replaced the Arabic script by a
modified Roman alphabet in an attempt to break the power of the
religious establishment and create a modern secular state out of the
old Ottoman Empire. His reform was successful for a number of
reasons: Arabic had truly been unsuitable for the Turkish language,
Turkish-speaking people living beyond Turkey's northern border
in Soviet Republics had already abandoned Arabic for Latinised
forms of the alphabet, and, last but not least, Ataturk had dictatorial
powers which enabled him to see that his decision was
implemented. Today, from an illiteracy rate of 90%, Turkey has
become on a par with the rest of Western Europe.

'The creation of a new writing system can, however, also be
motivated by a desire to assert one's own ethnic identity. In the
19th century a number of scripts evolved among what were often
tribal societies in parts of Africa and America. Invented mostly by
local people vaguely knowledgeable with the alphabetic mode of
writing, such creations were a part of a self-respect movement.
The majority of these scripts were short-lived; neither their
inventors nor the communities they served had the political or
economic resources to back up the invention. The most successful
systems were the Cherokee script, created by a Cherokee Indian,
Sikwayi, in the 1820s, and the so-called Alaskan script, invented by
the Eskimo Neck (1860-1924) with a group of assistants. Both are
still in use.

'Finally political considerations can also play a role within one
and the same writing system. The Roman alphabet, which spread
over Europe with Christianity, soon lost its uniform appearance
and split into a number of so-called 'national hands', mirroring the
break of the Western Roman Empire. In the 12th century one
particular style, the Gothic script, developed out of the Carolingian
miniscule; with the advent of printing in the 15th century this style
became the main system used for writing and printing in Germany.
Indeed, in Germany, traditions based on Gothic continued long
after the English Round Hand had become the established business
script. Nationals living in states absorbed by the Austro-Hungarian
Empire were forced to learn, and use, this script (together with the
German language) if they wished to take up posts in the

administration. In fact, in many Austrian schools children were first taught Gothic and then the Roman alphabet until well into the middle of the 20th century, creating the problems normally associated with acquiring a second writing system for no practical purpose at all.'

The history and development of Korean *Hangul*

Valerie Yule's involvement in many of the areas that interest me is evident in the references to her work in Sassoon (1993). Her recent PhD thesis (Yule 1991), *Orthographic factors in reading: spelling and society*, provides more examples of the social and political consequences of the reform of writing systems. Of Korean she writes in an informed way as she has lived in Korea and was able to observe the transition, and discover for herself how easy *Hangul* was to learn and use. She reports: 'Korean orthography has a history of politics, nationalism, elitism and pragmatic economics. It shows a transition made without difficulty, expense or fuss between two writing systems that are very different in their script and principles of language representation.

'In the first Korean orthographic reform, the benevolent medieval King Sejong sent a committee of scholars abroad to study other writing systems and to consult experts. They then, with characteristic spirit of independence, invented their own ingenious system, proclaimed in 1443, named according to their King's noble aims, *Hunmin-jongum*, 'Correct pronunciation of letters for teaching ordinary people'. On his death, the ruling mandarins suppressed the new writing system because they said, in alarm, it would enable the common people to read and write. Their power as an elite was bound up with the complex, difficult Chinese script and the scholarship it required. The great invention survived chiefly as the private script of the court ladies who had no classical education.

'In the nineteenth century, the revived and improved script with the fine title of *Hangul*, 'The Great Letters', was a nationalist symbol in the face of Chinese literary domination and Japanese conquest. Western traders and missionaries used it for easier communication and the missionary goal of popular education. Christianity has gained ground in Korea as in no other non-colonial Asian country.

'With the expulsion of the Japanese in 1945, *Hangul* gained official status, with popular enthusiasm, as it was both patriotic and easy – preferred over the internationally advantageous option of the Roman alphabet. North Korea now uses Hangul alone, but in the South the transition for the already literate was made by first using Hangul for the grammar and vocabulary not represented by Chinese characters (c.f. Japanese *Kana*). Mixed text is still common in the South because an acquaintance with Chinese *Hanja* is seen as useful for the many Chinese loan words and links with other Asian cultures. The spectacular rise in Korean literacy rates resulted from greater educational opportunities, the easy orthography for rapid independent reading and writing, plus national enthusiasm.'

Dr Yule explains that *Hangul*, sometimes called *Onmun*, is an alphabet, a syllabary and a logographic system together. It shows the ingenuity possible when a writing system and an orthography are carefully designed to be friendly to its users at every point, down to letter names that signify their sounds and the shape of the symbols designed to represent phonetic articulation. A Korean scholar in 1446 claimed that 'the bright can learn the system in a single morning and even the thick-headed can do so within ten days'. After reporting that foreign students, such as she, could learn it within a day, Valerie Yule explained how *Hangul* works: 'The

This reads: 'This is what English spelling might look like if it was written on the principles of Korean Hangul' (Yule, 1991).

simple 24 letters of the script, which represent the phonemes of the language, build up logically to make about 2000 mostly square-framed syllable blocks by stacking the geometric shapes of the consonants on to the basically bar shapes of the vowels.' She provides an example of what an English orthography based on Korean Hangul principles might look like.

Conclusions

These examples illustrate the variety of social and political issues reflected in handwriting. They range from purely pragmatic efforts to find a writing system to better suit a language, reflect national aspirations or open up a country to the wider world and improve literacy – to exactly the opposite. This might be the extinction of a separate religion or literary heritage at one extreme, or a desire to preserve an ancient culture at the other. Today there is another factor contributing to change. It is the difficulty in adapting certain writing systems for computer-generated communication. As a result their populations may be denied easy access to world knowledge and their nations may be cut off from trading opportunities.

白天鵝賓館

WHITE
SWAN
HOTEL

中國 廣州 沙面
SHAMIEN ISLAND
GUANGZHOU, CHINA
電話:86968 TELEPHONE:86968

CHAPTER 9

Typography and Handwriting

When printing was developing in Europe in the 15th century, the early typefaces mirrored the handwriting of the men who designed and made them – such as Aldus or Caxton. In other words, type became handwriting crystallised and formalised. If you go back a stage you can trace the personal or, more accurately, personal variations of the national hands in use in the various countries at that time and try to isolate what influenced such forms. The architecture and art of each of the countries might provide some clues – the soaring arches of Italy, the graceful lines of Botticelli – perhaps they were echoed in the letters of a sophisticated, educated elite and immortalised in the manuscripts of Arrighi or Tagliente.

These writing masters influenced early type design. As Lane and Daines (1992) put it: 'The Chancery hand, a calligraphic style refined to the highest level by the Italian writing masters in the fifteenth century, served as a model for the early development of italic typefaces. The most notable was the first italic type, by Aldus Minutius, which was produced in the first years of the sixteenth century.' According to Sutton and Bartram (1968): 'Only a few versions of Aldus's typefaces have been developed: but one, *Bembo*, makes up for this by its popularity as an extremely fine book face. *Bembo* is derived from Aldus's *De Aetna* Roman of 1495.' You are looking at it now. Bembo is the typeface used in this book.

The heavier Gothic styles of Flemish and German art and architecture are reflected in Gutenberg, and as Jean (1992) puts it: 'Analogies can be drawn between intersecting vaults and pointed arches of Gothic windows and forms of Gothic writing'. The much more homely, even crude, styles of the early typefaces of Caxton seem to reflect the shapes of oak beams in contemporary buildings. As time has passed type design has become international to a great extent, but the personality of the designer can still be seen in the character of some typefaces, just as it would be reflected in any other art form.

Opposite:
The design for the logo and name of the White Swan Hotel is designed to combine the two writing systems harmoniously. However the address below fails to live up to the rest of the page.

The connection between handwriting and typography

This word *typography* has had several definition in the past. As
Baudin (1989) so eloquently describes: 'Whether or not Gutenberg
was really the inventor we suppose him to have been, makes no
difference to the fact that what was invented was not a new
alphabet, or a new layout, but a method for multiplying identical
copies of any constellation of moveable type and any configuration
of text. This was not called *typography* by contemporaries. It was
called *the art of printing and writing without a pen.*'

Typography still works, to a certain extent, in the same way as
handwriting in that it reflects the user. More accurately, for other
than the type-designer himself, it is the choices that are made
which reflect and sometimes betray the user – subtle and elegant,
opulent and vulgar – whatever you choose when given a free
choice. In fairness, the subject or the client frequently dictate the
style to be used. The concept of a corporate identity uses type to
create exactly the right (or perceived) image for a company. The
skilled typographer uses type to create the mood required for any
particular purpose, while the packaging designer manipulates
letterforms and colour to influence the purchaser. Eventually it is
debatable who or what is being manipulated – the letterforms or
you, the reader or consumer.

This concept of how type creates an atmosphere, and how the
reader might react to it was perhaps best explored and explained by
Ovink in 1938. A more recent project was undertaken by two
Taiwanese researchers, Chuang and Cheng (1986).They explore
the psychological implications of Chinese typefaces. This study
took eight different typefaces and compared the similarities and
differences so as to provide guidelines for advertising layouts. The
typefaces used in this study are shown on the next page. The
method of testing readers' reaction to the typefaces was ingenious.
36 pairs of contrasting adjectives were used under four headings;

Attractiveness (boring – interesting, pleasant – unpleasant,
progressive – conservative)

Persuasiveness (convincing – unconvincing, dignified –
frivolous, fair – unfair)

Softness (friendly – unfriendly, feminine – masculine, hard – soft)

Elegance (crude – exquisite, immature – mature,
careful – careless).

The typefaces used in Chuang and Cheng's study (1986) which provided guidance for advertising and packaging designers.

Super-Bright	① 就和個不的得也在人耍
Super-Black	② 就和個不的得也在人要
Super-Round	③ 就和個不的得也在人要
Kai-Shu (formal)	④ 就和個不的得也在人要
Hsin-Shu (running)	⑤ 就和個不的得也在人要
Li-Shu (clerical)	⑥ 就和個不的得也在人要
Super-Round Decker	⑦ 就和個不的得也在人要
Hollow-Decker	⑧ 就和個不的得也在人要

The discussion sets out guidelines for the use of typefaces with different products, the purpose being to influence consumers and persuade them to buy. This fascinating and useful report leads the way in such research. It is interesting to note that it was undertaken by psychologists, not typographers.

With what might be termed multi-national advertising, typographers and graphic artists are being called on to make choices and to interpret typefaces relating to other writing systems. The way that the letterforms of the Latin alphabet are sometimes interpreted by those from other cultures can be illustrated in advertisements which have been subtly altered to reflect different tastes. The use of certain typefaces in advertising is also indicative of different tastes in other countries and is an interesting study in itself. This idea of manipulating specific characters to appeal to those of other cultures is spreading, sometimes going to extremes. I am even told that western-looking Japanese logos and corporate images are being designed purposely by non-Japanese graphic artists to appeal to non-Japanese consumers.

Combining two writing systems can work well (*(below)* in advertising. A combination of cultures in graphic form is not always a success (*right*).

NON-LATIN TYPEFACES

An illustration of typefaces produced by L'Imprimerie Nationale, Paris.

Typefaces and non-Latin scripts

Most writing systems can now be represented typographically and there is plenty to be learned from studying a library of non-Latin typefaces. I have one from Monotype Typography whose periodic publications have been a great help to me in my research. An even more diverse page from an advertisement from L'Imprimerie Nationale illustrates such delights as hieroglyphs and cuneiform typefaces, but there are still a few problems left to solve.

Eade (1993) reminds us that there are as yet no satisfactory ways of representing some languages, either in handwriting or typographically. His area of expertise lies in sub-Sahel Africa and he has provided this example of formatted Bassa text using the international phonetic alphabet. Even this alphabet, sometimes with several layers of diacritical marks, is inadequate to represent the subtleties of the various languages in the area, says Eade. He explained the problems that would arise with semi-skilled workers trying to produce printed material for basic literacy work. He put it this way: 'The grapheme-phoneme link is culturally arbitrary. Therefore two related languages with the same sound (phoneme) may not actually share the same grapheme.' He defined grapheme as a graphic representation of a phonetic sound. Eade continued: 'The responsibility for this decision would lie with the field linguists and therefore be conditioned by their training. It is this obvious weakness in the training of field linguists/translators/literacy workers that needs urgent attention'. To bring this unfamiliar state of affairs into focus, Eade likens it to the situation that might arise if literacy was being introduced into the UK for the first time in the same uncoordinated way. As he says: 'It is likely that vastly different alphabets, including complex diacritical arrangements, would be needed for Cockneys, Cornish or Cumbrian neo-literates.

I have a special interest in Fred Eade's work, as my own family of typefaces, Sassoon Primary, which is much used in literacy projects because of its clarity, is in the process of being extended. This work will take into account the additional characters needed to represent some of the languages Eade is researching.

Some other writing systems still cause a certain amount of difficulty. Although there are now Urdu typefaces, a newspaper from the late 1980s reports that a dozen calligraphers went on

Dèɓé gbù Sɔ́ɔ̀ dyúa

1 Sámìɔ 21:10-22:5

Ɓó tiaa ɓaɗaa, Dèɓé ɗú ma gbù kpàaì, ké ɔ mu ma ɗé Féɗésìà-hwɔ̀ɗɔ̀ ɓèɔ ɗò mú, ɗé káá mɔ̀ ma Ákìsì kɛɛ gbo. Ké gɔ̀mànà-nyɔ̀ ɓèɔ cɛ̄ɛ ma Ákìsì gbo, ké wa ɗá, "Má, Dèɓé mɔ̀ nyɔ kɔ̀ je wa dyià dyeeń nììn, wa ɓèɗèàìn mú, ɓé wa dyià níìń, 'Sɔ́ɔ̀ ɗà nyɔ táázîìn ɓè ɗáɓá, kɛɛ Dèɓé mɔ̀ɔ̀n ɗà táázîìn ɓaɗaa-bùè ɗáɓá' kɛɛ?" Ti ɓé Dèɓé wɔ́ ma wa wuɗuɔ̀ kɛɛ, ɔ fɛ̀ɛn ma káá ɔ dyi mìɔ. Ɔ jèɛɛ, ɔ nyu ma ɗɛ kà sàà-nyɔ̀ nyuà kɛ ɓó wa dyúa. Ti ɓé wa kpa ɱa ɔ káá ɔ gboɛɛ, ɔ céé ma hwɔɗɔɔ gmɔ-wɔ̀ɔ̀ kɔ̄ɛn, ké ɔ nyue ké tɔ̄ɔ dèèn ma ɔ vèɔ̀ mú. Ké Ákìsì cɛ̄ɛ ma ɔ gɔ̀mànà-nyɔ̀ ɓèɔ gbo, ké ɔ ɗá, "Ɓè gmɔ̀ ɗéa, gàaɔ̀ mɔ̀ sàà-nyɔ̀. Ɗé kɔ̀ je ɓè dyàà ɱ́ gboɛ́? Ɓè hwɔ̀ɗɔ̀ ɗá ɱ́ se nɔ̄ sàà-nyɔ̀ pàɗà ɓéɗéè?"

Sɔ̀ɔ̀èn ɓóɛɛ gboɛɛ, Dèɓé kpá ma xwáɗáán ɗe, ké ɔ mu ma ɗé ɓí ɗò mú. Ti ɓé ɔ ɗíígàà ɓèɔ wɔ́ɔ ma kà ɓé ɔ nì ma ɗéɛɛ, wa poeèn ma ɗé ɔ gbo dyí. Ké nyɔ ɓè ɓé wa nì ma gà dyéeń nyɛ kè nyɔ ɓè ɓé wa ɓéɗé ma wa muee ɗòè kpaa kè nyɔ ɓè kɔ̀ hwɔ̀ɗɔ̀ se ma dyi dèɛɛ mu ma ɗé Dèɓé gbo ɗekè. Wa séén ɓéèn ma kà gàa hɔ̄dèɗè hīinyɛ jùè, ké Dèɓé mɔ̀ ma wa nààìn-nyɔ̀.

This page is an excerpt from a children's story bible, in Bassa, a language spoken in Liberia. It was provided by Dr. Eade. He has a long-standing interest in vernacular text, in particular its use in literacy work and the readers' interaction with it.

strike in New Delhi as it says 'reminding the world that there is still one language that has eluded the typesetters – Urdu. Although experimental computer typesetting is being studied here and in Pakistan where Urdu is the national language, newspapers in both countries still rely on accomplished scribes called katibs.' The article goes on to describe how no more than a handful of Urdu newspapers survive in Delhi, and that the katibs, perched on wooden platforms in dingy back rooms, turn out their handwritten news columns at the rate of of about ten inches an hour. The 'type' then goes straight to photo–composition. The article ends on a more pragmatic issue 'Since 1968, when the court classified us as journalists, we have been cheated by the proprietors.'

I understand that at least until very recently, community newspapers written in Urdu, in London were produced in the

There are still several languages, across the Sahel (sub-Sahara Africa) for whom the Latin based character set does not offer a satisfactory solution to representing their language. 'Even a judicious use of the International Phonetic Alphabet leads to inconsistencies' says Eade. He also noted that, sadly, the linkage of writing system to language is often a political or religious decision, not necessarily resulting in the most suitable alphabet for any particular language.

The letter A, with metric lines and sub-fitting characters superimposed. (Lofting, 1992)

same way – by hand. However, anything written on this subject risks being out of date before being published itself.

Undoubtedly many projects are in hand, all over the world, to bring up to date those writing systems not yet easily typeset. Peter Lofting recently undertook one such project over three years. This was the typographic analysis and and font design for one of the most complex calligraphic scripts still use in the world. The script was Tibetan and and the typographic analysis was part of a larger collaborative project, working with other language scholars and programmers, to computerize the script for the Royal Government of Bhutan. As Lofting (1992) describes: 'The language of Bhutan is Dzongkha and the script used to write it derived from the classical Tibetan monastic letterforms called U-chen.

The writing of both Dzongkha and Tibetan is syllabic. The thirty consonant characters and four vowel marks are written in combinations to represent 8000 different syllables.' Lofting continues: 'Complexity arises because the syllable combinations are mostly written vertically in conjoint stacks, in very much the same way that mathematical fractions are built up – though in this case they are equations of sound. In this way more than 600 vertical stack combinations can occur in the script. In addition, when combining vertically, many letters change their form or proportion. 'This creates a formidable design task for the typographer, who has to balance the conflicting need for modularity with that of calligraphic sublety.'

Bengali letterforms and typesetting

Trilokesh Mukherjee talked to me about Bengali letterforms in relation to typesetting and design. He said: 'Like most languages of the world, the spoken and written forms in the Bengali language had already developed before the coming of printing (brought by the Europeans during the fourth quarter of the 18th century). The printing types began to give letterforms the usual structural rigidity that the solidity of the metal gives. This shackle was not broken until the fourth quarter of this century.'

From the Sanskrit language and the Devanagari script, Bengali has received most of its uniqueness and problems. We will discuss them briefly in relation to typography. (Comments that Mukherjee made in relation to handwriting appear in Chapter 6.)

The Matra

Bengali writing does not stand on an invisible baseline. It hangs
from an visible horizontal rule known as a matra. It is the most
important aspect of the letterform. The numbers have no matra.
The absence and the presence of the matra can alter the letterform
e.g. এ ay or এ় tra. In Sanskrit matra means measure. In this
context it can be explained that each letter has been given a space
value by the horizontal rules under the letter. For the first type-
designers of Bengali, the understanding and the use of the matra
became a valuable asset.

The Bengali letterforms

There are five different forms of the letters used in the Bengali
writing system:

    Vowels
    Consonants
    Diacritical marks
    Joint letters

(For handwriting as different from the typeface see page 85.) There
is no concept of x height in the Bengali letterforms. Neither has it
any conceptual understanding of a capital letter or an upper case
and lower case. However what it does share with many letterforms
of the Indian sub-continent is the concept of letter-height (space
between the visible matra and the invisible baseline) and the letter
width. This is important as most diacritical marks are normally
added to the letters either above, below, to the right or to the left
of the letter in a predetermined way.

Typeface nomenclature
for the Bengali script,
from Ross (1989).

It is not only in Indian scripts that these problems arise. Barden (1991) reviewed the presentations on non-Latin typography from the multinational gathering of Typ 90 in Oxford, where Ari Davidow contributed his specialised knowledge, saying: 'The question that faced Hebrew typographers with the invention of printing was how to take the calligraphic forms and move them into print.' He expanded the subject to consider the difficulties of multi-lingual settings, in his case with two writing systems reading in two different directions. He also said that he felt that non-Latin typefaces should not be treated as if the world were some kind of biligual entity, with Latin type – and English in particular – constituting a permanent half of the equation. Davidow (1993) expanded on this theme in considerable detail adding: 'We need not only to develop tools for working with single languages in all the complexities of their traditional forms, we also need to develop tools and forms that facilitate the presentation of languages together.' This is the challenge we now must face if we are to bring together the languages of our world in equal partnership.

Who should design typefaces?
I would like to float a few controversial ideas here. How much are other countries over-influenced by Western concepts of typography? 'Bold', 'italic', 'serifed' are all terms that relate to the Latin alphabet but which have been transferred to other cultures and their letterforms. It seems, for instance, incongruous to find the word Grotesque in conjunction with a Kanji typeface, or as Ross (1989) records, Indian versions of Univers. Should such terms and the concepts that they embody be imposed on other cultures?

This leads on to another subject that interests me and has a certain relevance to the inferences made in this chapter – that of the design of typefaces for use in other cultures. It seems to me that sensitivity to the cultural heritage is just as important as type design expertise when it comes to designing characters for another writing system. Now that technology is more or less universal, I would like to see some comparative studies into the subtle differences in typefaces designed by nationals of a particular culture and those from without it. I know that in some countries, India in particular, feelings that Indian typefaces should be designed by

Indian nationals are particularly strong. I have tried to find
designers from other countries who are willing to say what they
really feel about this subject, but I have found everyone too polite
(so far). A Japanese friend, who is a well-known type-designer,
went so far as to say that he was pretty sure that he would be able
to tell if a typeface had been designed by a Japanese designer or a
European – and there is no shortage of excellent Japanese type
designers today, as the results of a recent international type design
contest illustrate.

I feel that to manipulate letters you must know them intimately:
how you can simplify them, elaborate on them, twist their forms
and not only retain their recognisability but their spirit as well.
Then you need the expertise to draw them accurately – but maybe
that is of lesser importance, or should I say, more a widely
attainable skill. What worries me, as I dig ever deeper into the
implications of personal and national forms of letters, is this very
matter of cultural heritage. Surely it would be better if those who
design typefaces should be able to write the alphabet or characters
involved – and have an understanding of the culture to which it
belongs and a sensitivity to all these matters. It can of course go
further, as my good friend Briem says: 'Europeans misunderstand
and wrongly modify Arabic, and Eric Gill's Hebrew is a prime
example of someone imposing his own concepts of serifs
somewhat arrogantly on another cultures letterforms.'

אבגדרהוזחטיכרלמ
קץצפפעסנום
(.,?!";:)רשׁתּת

An example of Gill
Hebrew alphabet.

Fiona Ross, whose first training was as a linguist and is an expert
on Indian typefaces, summed up for me what she feels on this
subject: 'I do not believe that it is possible to design a satisfactory

typeface unless the designer (or a member of the design team) is fully conversant with the writing system being translated into type. Non-Latin scripts are not simply decorations on a page. The designer needs to be aware of the significance of any shape to recognise, for instance, whether a loop is an embellishment, a regional variation, or an essential distinguishing element; s/he should also perceive how letterforms relate to each other to form a cohesive design that is immediately intelligible (at least in text faces) to the reader.'

Fiona Ross had long expressed strong views on this subject. In 1989 she wrote of the situation:

> The most recent technology of desk-top publishing has placed fount-manufacturing tools in the hands of almost every personal-computer user, i.e. type design is now available to the non-professional designer. The result has been a rash of non-Latin founts, the majority of which are second-rate copies of well-known designs. Plagiarism has increased considerably.... Nevertheless the current situation should be welcomed. Periods of imitation eventually give way to innovation. The possibilities available to the designers of Indian typefaces have never been greater; letterforms and typographic refinements that were not feasible in metal can be produced as digital letterforms.... The indigenous tradition of penned or printed letterforms can inspire new typefaces by designers who appreciate the inherent complexities of Indian scripts and recognise that there is no quick-and-easy route to producing founts of enduring quality.

Choices

It would be interesting to know what typefaces readers from other cultures, if presented with a representative choice, would relate to best, or find easiest to read (either in their own writing system and language, or in any other). Two unrelated instances suggest that research would be likely to produce some interesting results. Firstly, the decided way that many Chinese students proclaimed that (admittedly to write rather than to read) copperplate was more aesthetic a style than italic, see page 92, and secondly my own work reported in *Computers and Typography* (1993) on the

TERMINALS OF CHINESE TYPEFACES

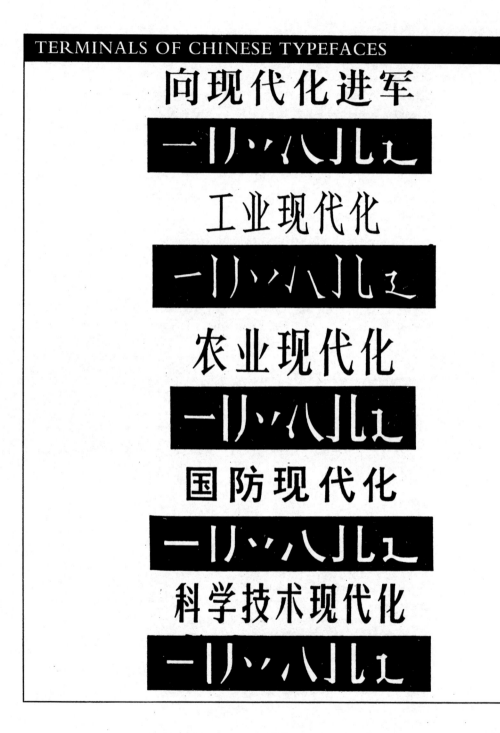

preferences that children showed for particular elements of typefaces. This family of typefaces has been well received in their country of origin, Great Britain, as well as in the United States, Australia and South Africa to name but a few, but has had quite different reactions from the French and Italians. Several sources have reported that the letterforms did not conform to their idea of what children would relate to or prefer to read, because of the longstanding cultural differences to the concept of letterforms. I believe that this is much more than just the influence of different handwriting models, which some people have suggested.

I know of no studies that have considered these attitudes cross-culturally. My own experience has suggested to me that so-called experts have, for far too long, pontificated on what they consider suitable, whether for different ages, different nationalities using the same writing system or more importantly for those from different cultures, without ever researching to see what the truth of the matter might be.

More details of the terminals for Chinese typefaces from the same source as opposite, Meishuzi (1980).

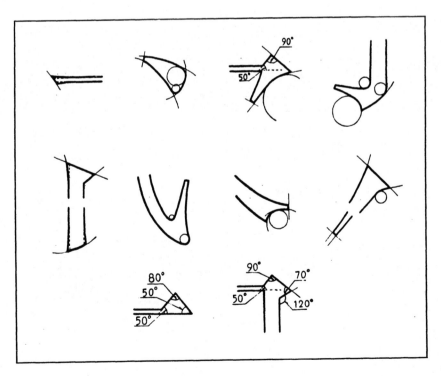

计算机激光汉字精密照排系统

计算机激光汉字精密照排系统

计算机激光汉字精密照排系统

计算机激光汉字精密照排系统

计算机激光汉字精密照排系统

计算机激光汉字精密照排系统

计算机激光汉字精密照排系统

计算机激光汉字精密照排系统

计算机激光汉字精密照排系统

计算机激光汉字精密照排系统

计算机激光汉字精密照排系统

计算机激光汉字精密照排系统

计算机激光汉字精密照排系统

计算机激光汉字精密照排系统

计算机激光汉字精密照排系统

计算机激光汉字精密照排系统

计算机激光汉字精密照排系统

计算机激光汉字精密照排系统

计算机激光汉字精密照排系统

CHAPTER 10

Computers and handwriting

Traditional typography and computer generated letters are by now inextricably entangled. The idea of typography as exclusively a professional area is being eroded. In *Computers and Typography* (Sassoon 1993) the contributors all stressed that the lessons of five centuries of typographic study should not be ignored, but that is not the point in question here. It is the use of the computer in education and daily life, particularly in the multi-cultural field, that is relevant. Some of the issues involved in education by computer are being questioned, quite rightly, before it is too late. Do we learn something vital by physically writing out words, or will we eventually do just as well via the screen and the keyboard? Then we should ask whether the advantage of having encyclopaedic information at everyone's finger tip on a CD will lead to the need for restrictions to ensure that the information is assimilated rather than simply being copied and printed out. Electronic books may sound an economic and logical extension of the use of computers in education, but unless due care is taken about letterforms and spacing, and simple navigational aids are developed, they could become an expensive experiment, and at worst, create visual problems for their users.

From a slightly different viewpoint, we need to consider whether creative writers produce equally imaginative work directly on the computer, or does writing by hand involve the writer more in the emotion that they are trying to express? Another question that is now becoming evident as the initial euphoria surrounding the use of computers in schools subsides: 'How successfully do we judge work (our own as well as other people's), when the presentation looks professional?' In other words are our eyes deceived and our judgement swayed because the reader has to make less effort to decipher the content? There are those who think that too much technology may get in the way of learning and that computers may have already played a part in de-skilling our children. If teaching of literacy is to become technological, we must ensure that teachers (i.e technologists) are themselves fully literate in the widest sense.

Opposite:
Two typefaces designed in Beijing for use on laserprinters. They are legible even when reproduced at very small point sizes.

Keeping a balanced attitude to computers

There are other questions to ask about the increasing use of
computers as a writing tool in education before we can make a
balanced judgements. Computers work within a framework that
controls what they can accept and what they cannot. There is a
danger in imposing on people's thinking a computer compatible
framework. Where, in certain circumstances, memory is replaced
by an outside database, the choice of extracts may still be
intellectual and original, but the basic matter is not. In this way the
mind may be bent or limited by the material available to it.

There is also a worry that many decisions today are commercially
rather than intellectually led. The use of computers is increasing in
schools worldwide and along with this the use of computer assisted
learning (CAL). Take, for example, software to assist in the
compositional aspect of writing. Honest and balanced appraisal is
needed to ensure that while this may benefit reluctant writers, it
does not have the opposite effect on creative communicators. As
more sensitive interactive educational software is developed it may
well take over much of the assessment of pupils' progress – a
welcome idea in that it will remove subjective judgements and
presumably save time, but worrying all the same. It will require
highly intelligent programming to fit the needs, and follow the
thinking, of the more intelligent and imaginative of our students.

Do we still need handwriting?

Nobody doubts the advantages of computers for those whose
handicaps had previously prevented them from communicating,
but what about the general populace? Those of us who talk about
handwriting are asked the same question by almost every audience:
'Why bother to teach handwriting any more at all?' It is not easy
to answer that question – though economic forces will delay the
day when computers might take over entirely in education in
many parts of the world. The real question is whether supplanting
handwriting by the computer entirely might be a good idea or not.
My own feeling is that to make your mark is a human instinct –
something not to be lightly denied or dismissed, and that there will
always be a need for handwriting. If we deny the skill to some
parts of the populace on the increasingly alluring (usually
commercially-led) promise of saving teaching time, then we will

eventually end up with a two tier populace. Those who can write by hand as well as use the computer will be at the top, and those who can only use a keyboard will be disadvantaged. Between those two statements there is plenty of room for compromise. Undoubtedly today, with the requirement of speed as well as legibility and an ever-increasing need for note-taking in education and later life as well, we are asking our hands to perform a job for which they were not designed. Hence the increase of writer's cramp worldwide. Many jobs are best performed by a computer, and the sooner that they are generally available in schools worldwide the better – but not for all tasks. My own belief, at present, is that those who are physically able to write should not be put onto a computer in any way that destroys their confidence in their own handwriting. However we must think about the new possibilities for personal and international communication that the new technology is opening up.

It is now time to extend the idea of communication from the hand to the keyboard in a multi-cultural context. As a bilingual adult, and a professional computer user, Ari Davidow is in a good position to extol the use of technology in this area. He brings in yet another perspective. He reports on his own experience in *Computers and Typography* (1993). 'When I was a child and we spoke both Hebrew and English around the house, we had only an English typewriter. We never procured one for Hebrew.' He relates how his high school papers were neatly typed, and that to him, the handwritten page lacks the authority of one that is neatly typewritten. His papers for religious school had to be written by hand, which he says was torture for him. 'Partly as a consequence, it was not until the computer age was sufficiently advanced for me to encounter programs that enabled me to type in Hebrew that I began to study the language seriously.'

Chris Abbott has contributed the next section, describing his multi-lingual word-processing project. He tells of the part that it can play in giving those who have had to adapt to the language and writing of an adopted country access to, and a pride in their first language and culture. He reports on a project developed initially for London schools but with implications for many countries where school children (and adults) may be adapting to a second writing system as well as a second language.

How computers are finally beginning to support the multilingual subject

Although still ashamedly monolingual myself, I have spent many years in an environment where one language, English, has been pre-eminent and status-laden, and where other languages, often first languages of the people I have worked with, have been definitely less valued. Since my career gradually caused me to become more involved with computers, I was interested in what these machines might offer at least to attempt to even out this imbalance. I found little to enthuse about until I came across Allwrite, a multilingual word processor developed by the Inner London Education Authority before its abolition. Since I later worked at ILECC, where the program was developed, and later still became its Director, I have been able to be closely involved with the development of computer access to languages other than English.

Allwrite is a word processor which can handle a wide range of languages with different scripts. It is designed to be simple to use, and has its own large fonts which can be printed out in four sizes. It was developed in response to needs in London schools, where as many as one hundred and seventy-six languages have been recorded as being in use. With the average London classroom being a multilingual one, it was vital to develop word-processing facilities in as many languages as possible. The program was released in 1988 and won a British Design Award in 1991. Although the first version of the program was written for the RM Nimbus computer, found in many schools, Allwrite 2, released in 1993, is available for the IBM-compatible PC.

Chris Abbott who was Director of ILECC (Inner London Educational Computer Centre) has contributed this section. Sadly ILECC was disbanded in 1994, shortly after this was written. Chris Abbott is now a senior research fellow at the Centre for Educational Studies, Kings College, London.

The development of Allwrite

The program was developed by a local authority education centre because it would not otherwise exist. As Marshall (1992) has noted: 'The collapse of national computer industries and the overwhelming influence of the USA has meant that, until recently, consideration of any language other than English was of little commercial value. After all, doesn't *everyone* in computing speak English?'

A useful by-product of the development has been the interaction between programmers and language teachers, a pairing that is unusual considering the divide between the arts and the sciences. In particular, a mutual respect has developed at ILECC between programmers and designers and the representatives of the language communities, who are always involved in the development of a new character set. It has sometimes been necessary to have long and complex discussions about appropriate letterforms where there is no common agreement across cultural groups sharing the same language or character set. Despite this, it has always been possible to reach eventual compromise and thus meet the criticism put forward by Williams (1993) that 'it is rare to find software that has paid much attention to the writer's perception of the task. Rather it pays attention to the designer's perception of the writer's task.'

Although the languages supported were previously written with a pen, a brush or some other specialised implement, the use of the computer forces the selection of a common tool. In most cases this means the mouse, although some adult users prefer to use the keyboard, especially if they have previously used a computer in English. Since it has always been the intention that Allwrite should be a multilingual package, an early decision was taken that all necessary word-processing operations should be achieved in exactly the same way, whatever the language in use. For most of the available languages it is possible to choose to have screen messages in the language in use or in English.

Phrases such as SAVE TEXT or REPLACE WITH can appear in Bengali, Gujerati or Panjabi, for example, according to the language in use. This is often desirable but problems can be caused by the language interference that English exerts on other tongues. There may be a Bengali phrase for SAVE FILE but if most Bangla speakers use the English phrase, it may be that it is not sensible to reverse this. One early outcome of more recent work with adults has been the discovery that many of them prefer the messages in English. Children, on the other hand, delight in seeing their own language used on the screen, and often teach their classmates how to recognise 'Yes' and 'No' in the language in question in order to confirm operations.

Interest and attitudes from other countries
The addition of an IBM compatible version has meant that interest has arisen in a number of other countries. There are considerable

differences in attitude, however, and these are obviously related to
national attitudes to mother tongue maintenance and the perceived
need to maintain what some see as the purity of the national
language. Teachers from Germany and France have queried the
desirability of offering any other language on the computer,
whereas countries such as Sweden and Denmark have a very
different attitude. The Swedish position is probably the most
progressive one, where there is a requirement for schools to
support and maintain the first language of their students.

Adapting to different writing systems
The languages currently offered by Allwrite fall into several main
groups. The first to be developed were the South Asian languages,
particularly those spoken in the London area. Among these are
Bengali, Gujerati, Hindi, Panjabi and Tamil. The program can also
handle languages that need to be written from right to left, and
those so far available are Arabic, Farsi and Urdu. Urdu was a
particular problem as it proved impossible to produce a satisfactory
Nastaliq font, and the one currently available is Nasq, a
compromise that most users have accepted given the very low cost
of the program. A variety of fonts for each language is a future aim
and has already been achieved for Gujerati. If English writers can
use bold, italic and underlined phrases or different point sizes to
achieve impact or improve communication, then writers of other
languages should be able to do the same.

An interesting development with the right to left languages has
been the realisation that what might be a drawback to the program
is actually a benefit in some circumstances. Many sophisticated and
expensive word-processing programs for languages such as Arabic
use intelligent algorithms to select the appropriate form of a
character, depending on its location within the word. Allwrite, on
the other hand, simply provides the user with a bank of initial,
medial and final forms, and the user has to know which one is
required. This slows down a competent user but teachers of
languages have said that this is exactly what is needed for learners,
who would have to make such a decision if handwriting was being
produced. The computer not only removes the need to remember
the exact form, it offers a bank of letterforms from which to
choose.

Supporting the bilingual writer

Work in schools has led to a greater understanding of the way in which word-processing can support bilingual writing, especially where the first language is other than English. Many schools have used the program as a bridge to their local communities, involving mother and toddler groups or parent-teacher organisations in the production of labels, signs and traditional stories in several languages. One case study found that an early action prompted in young children, offered access to the program, was to write letters to their parents. Children who were hesitant about their ability to write in Bengali felt much more confident when the characters from which they needed to select were visible on the screen. It was reported in Kemeny (1990) that: 'The video which recorded the process revealed that all four had been involved in the actual word-processing, rather than one child scribing for the non-writers. They could all be seen searching for the right characters – touching the screen and reaching over each other to use the keyboard... and they were all sharing in the composition.'

Work with parents more recently has resulted in requests from them that they be given time to write with their children. Such families are constructing and reinforcing their complex linguistic structures through the use of multilingual word-processing. Parents have also shown collaborative strategies when writing with computers, even where these are culturally more constrained through the gender or cultural mix evident on a particular occasion. It has been of particular interest that girls and women have shown great interest and enthusiasm in the program, even to the extent of becoming trainers of older male adults. This has even been the case within cultures where this might not have been thought likely.

If English is in future to be produced and mediated through the use of computers, then it is vital that other languages should be enabled to use the same medium. The predominance of English must be challenged and other languages enabled, as they will be by such projects as that concerning the new Unicode standards. The understanding is there, as is the recognition of the current imbalance: all that remains to be acquired is the will to change. It is in our schools that we see change happening and this must be a good sign for the future of all of us.'

Before leaving his work, I would like to add a comment that I heard Abbott make recently at a lecture. It concerned the importance of balancing the size and weight of different typefaces when more than one writing system is in use. This in itself is not easy, but he felt that having one heavier or larger seems to give that language more prominence in the mind of the reader

Conclusion

Abbott has illustrated how children (and even adults), torn between two cultures, are vulnerable wherever they may be in the world. Where computers can help, they should be encouraged. With adults in particular, the computer has the added function of hiding the inadequate handwriting that is often the result of hesitancy in a second language or writing system. The use of technology might give status as well as confidence to learners in the community.

The effect of computers on writing systems, and on international communication in general, expands the subject considerably. New developments in other forms of graphic communication such as Braille, deaf-signing notation and movement or music notation have come about as a result of recent developments in computer technology. When various other iconic systems used in special needs, for example, are included, a further need for international cooperation is revealed. Icons, for instance, for whatever purpose, can cross language barriers, but need to be standardised, and culturally acceptable, if they are to work for everyone.

I hope that this part of the book will alert those not yet conversant with the ever more advanced technology to the possibilities that there are for multi-lingual and multi-media communication in so many areas. At the same time, those involved in computer technology need to remember the effects and implications of the written trace. They must take into account the very real cultural differences towards certain aspects of graphic communication which cannot be expected to disappear overnight.

Bibliography

Al-Haideri B. (1981). Influences and factors in the development of Arabic Calligraphy in *Arabic Calligraphy*, eds. Saggar M., Alani G., and Dhanoon Y., Iraqi Cultural Centre.

Boston R. (1989). *Osbert - A Portrait of Osbert Lancaster.* Collins.

Brown M. (1990). *A Guide to Western Historic Scripts, from Antiquity to 1600.* British Library.

Butterworth B. and Yin W. (1991). The universality of two routines for reading: evidence from Chinese dyslexia. *Proc. R. Soc.* London B 245 91-5.

Chuang C.J. and Cheng B.S. (1986). The psychological meaning of Chinese typography and its application in advertising. In *Linguistics, Psychology and the Chinese Language*, eds. Kao H.S.R.and Hoosain R., University of Hong Kong.

Cooper R. (1994). Look before the pencil leaps. In *Notes on Literacy.* Summer Institute of Linguistics, Texas.

David I. (1990). *The Hebrew Letter.* Jason Aronson, New Jersey.

Diringer D. (1962). *Writing.* Thames and Hudson.

Driver G.R. (1948). *Semitic Writing.* Published for the British Academy by Oxford University Press.

Dunn O. (1984). Beginning handwriting in English with children who already write in a different script. In *World Language English,* vol. 4, no. 1, Pergamon Press Ltd.

Eade F. (1992). Non-Latin script directory: Didot can play a Part. *Didot Bulletin* No 2.

Eade F. (1993). *The graphic language of vernacular literacy primers in West Africa.* Thesis for the Degree of Doctor of Philosophy, Dept. of Typography & Graphic Communication, University of Reading.

Eade F. (1994). Lobis, lasers and literacy. In *Notes on Literacy.* Summer Institute of Linguistics, Texas.

Fayer M. (1987). *Simplified Russian Grammar.* National Textbook Co., Lincolnswood, Illinois.

Fok A. and Bellugi U. (1986). The acquisition of a visual spatial script. In *Graphonomics*, eds Kao H.S.R. van Galen G.P. and Hoosain R., North Holland.

Gaur A. (1979). *Writing Materials of the East.* British Library.

Gaur A. (1984). *A History of Writing.* British Library.

Gaur A. (1994). *A History of Calligraphy.* British Library.

Goodnow J. (1977). *Children's Drawing.* Fontana.

Gordon V.E.C. and Mock R. (1960). *Twentieth Century Handwriting.* Methuen.

Jacoby H.J. (1939). *Analysis of Handwriting.* Allen and Unwin.

Jean G (1992). *Writing.* Thames and Hudson.

Kemeny H. (1990). *Talking IT Through.* NCET.

Harris R. (1986). *The Origin of Writing.* Duckworth.

Kao H.S.R. and Hoosain R.(1986). *Linguistics Psychology and the Chinese Language.* University of Hong Kong.

Kao H.S.R. and Hoosain R.(1984). *Psychological Studies of the Chinese Language.* University of Hong Kong.

Lane J. and Daines M. (1992). Glossary in *26 Letters.* An Annual and Calendar produced by ATypI.

Lieblich A. and Ninio A. (1960). *Developmental trends in directionality of drawings in Jewish and Arab children*. Journal of Cross-cultural Psychology.

Lofting P. (1992). *From Bamboo Quill to Laser.* ESND (European Society for News Design) News, no 5, May.

Lurçat L (1985). *L'Écriture et la Langage Écrit de L'Enfant.* Les Éditions ESF.

Marshall L.F. (1992). Internationalisation: the programmer, the user and the writer. *In Computers and Writing: State of the Art,* eds. Williams and Holt. Intellect.

Menasse–Cremer M-J. (1992). *Chinese Graphology the Precursors, Current Research and Prospects.* International Institute for Scientific Research into Chinese Graphology.

Monotype (1993). *Library of Non-Latin Typefaces.* Monotype Typography Ltd.

Naveh J. (1975). *Origins of the Alphabet.* Cassell.

Nihei Y. (1992). Handwriting as a social act: The rise and fall of an anti-calligraphic style of handwriting in Japan. Presented at the 25th International Congress of Psychology, Brussels.

Ovink GW (1938). *Legibility, Atmosphere-value and Forms of Printing,* A.W. Sijthoff's Uit Geversmaatschappij N.V..

Peer L. (1991). Bilingualism and Dyslexia. *PATTOS Journal,* April.

Safadi Y. H. (1978). *Islamic Calligraphy.* Thames and Hudson.

Sassoon J. (1990). Who on earth invented the alphabet? In *Visible Language,* vol. XXIV no. 2.

Sassoon R. (1991). *Handwriting Book* in *Children's English.* Linguaphone Institute Ltd.

Sassoon R and Lovett P. (1992). *Creating Letterforms.* Thames and Hudson.

Sassoon R. (1993). *The Art and Science of Handwriting*. Intellect.

Sassoon R. (1993). *Computers and Typography*. Intellect.

Sutton J. and Bartram A. (1968). *An Atlas of Typeforms*. Lund Humphries.

Virágvölgyi P. (1978). *Javaslat az Irástanitás Reformjára*. Magyar Iparmüvészeti Föiskola, Budapest.

Virágvölgyi P. (1978). *A Maci Ir*, a copybook for Hungarian schools. Magyar Iparmüvészeti Föiskola, Budapest.

Williams N (1992). New Technology, New Writing, New Problems? In *Computers and and Writing: State of the Art*, eds Williams N. and Holt P., Intellect.

Yule V. (1991). *Orthographic Factors in Reading: Spelling and Society*. Thesis submitted for the degree of Doctor of Philosophy, Faculty of Education, Monash University, Vic. Australia.

Index